Decision-making in
the European Community

For Joanna, Tristan and Stefan

Decision-making in the European Community

The Council Presidency and European integration

Emil Joseph Kirchner

Manchester University Press
Manchester and New York
Distributed exclusively in the USA and Canada by St. Martin's Press

Published by Manchester University Press
Oxford Road, Manchester M13 9PL, UK
and Room 400, 175 Fifth Avenue, New York, NY 10010, USA

Distributed exclusively in the USA and Canada
by St. Martin's Press, Inc., 175 Fifth Avenue, New York,
NY 10010, USA

Reprinted in hardback and paperback 1992.

A catalogue record for this book is available from the British Library

Library of Congress cataloging in publication data
Kirchner, Emil Joseph.
    Decision-making in the European community : the council presidency
and European integration / Emil Joseph Kirchner.
        p.   cm.
    Includes bibliographical references and index.
    ISBN 0–7190–3173–7
    1. European Economic Community.   European Council.   2. European
federation. I. Title.
JN15.K548   1992
341.24′22—dc20   91–4332

ISBN 0 7190 3173 7 *hardback*
ISBN 0 7190 3996 7 *paperback*

Typeset in Great Britain
by Northern Phototypesetting Co. Ltd., Bolton
Printed in Great Britain
by Redwood Press Ltd, Melksham

Contents

Tables and figures

Tables

Figure

Preface

The dynamics of the internal market, regime changes in Eastern Europe and the inadequate handling of the Gulf conflict provided the European Community with an opportunity to take major strides towards greater integration in the 1990s. As in previous periods greater integration confronts national interests which so far have been the main determinants of the speed and direction of integration. However, unlike the past, when the Community progressed in fits and starts, there are now significant practices in EC decision-making, (like the 'mutual recognition' of national standards and 'subsidiarity'), which smooth the links between Community and national competences and which promote a 'pooling of sovereignties' among the member states. There is now an interlocking between national and Community administrations and a symbiotic decision-making relationship between national and Community institutions. This reduces member states' fears of either losing too much power too quickly or creating a heavily centralised and bureaucratised EC machinery.

Interstate bargains, the carrying out of 'joint tasks' between national and Community institutions and the 'pooling of sovereignties' will, therefore, be characteristic of EC decision-making in the 1990s. The Community, pressed by internal and external demands, will proceed in a way which is analogous to confederal or 'co-operative federal' decision-making practices. Internally, the Community will have to establish common policies in such fields as economic, monetary, social and environment, in order to reap the fruits of the internal market and to secure social and economic cohesion. Externally, the Community is faced with the question of enlargement, which has direct bearings on efforts to 'deepen' integration. It also has to develop a common foreign and security policy in order to meet American demands for more self-reliance and to produce a common and responsible approach to international developments (for example, in Eastern Europe and the Middle East).

A major concern of the EC has been how to respond adequately to internal and external pressures with an appropriate combination of EC policy provisions, institutional innovations, decision-making effectiveness and democratic control. This was not only a problem for the negotiators involved in the two Intergovernmental Conferences on EMU and Political Union in 1991, (which were still in progress at the time when this manuscript was finalised) but appeared likely to affect the EC agenda for the remaining decade. The overriding objective was how to strike a balance between EC task expansion and the maintenance of national control or identity.

Governments and government leaders will continue to play a major role in the shaping of Community development. Much of their impact will continue to be channelled via the Council of Ministers and the European Council, and closely involves the role of the rotating Council Presidency. The centrality of the Council Presidency in EC decision-making, and its role in the implementation of the Single European Act and in EC integration generally, was the main subject of investigation in this book. Different approaches to the study of integration were a second focus. The objective was to determine which of the approaches is most relevant for explaining developments such as the SEA and the two Intergovernmental Conferences on EMU and Political Union, and the future of the nation state.

The empirical study was made possible by a small research grant from the British Academy and by a research grant from the ESRC (No. R 000 23 1595) which allowed me to relinquish my University teaching duties for one year and to undertake field work in a number of EC countries. I am most grateful to these institutions, as well as the Commission of the EC for their financial assistance.

I have benefited from the very valuable time a great number of diplomats and government officials in eight national capitals granted me to discuss the role and impact of the Council Presidency. Their 'first-hand' knowledge of how the Presidencies work and contribute to decision-making as well as to integration was of immense help to me in comparing and assessing the importance of this Community actor. I would like to thank them sincerely both for their information and co-operation. My gratitude extends also to civil servants in the Secretariats of the Council of Ministers and the European Parliament as well as to the diplomats in the EPC Secretariat who provided me with valuable information and statistical material.

Several individuals were kind enough to comment on drafts in the writing of this book. In particular, I would like to thank Kevin Featherstone, Mike Mills and Elinor Scarbrough who read the entire draft manuscript and made insightful suggestions for its improvement. Simon Bulmer, Richard Corbett, John Fitzmaurice, John Peterson and Hugh Ward commented expertly on individual draft chapters. A word of thanks is also due to Hilary Doughty for her help in compiling the data on national elections and government changes and to Alfonso Nunez for his assistance in the general collection of documentation.

My greatest debt is to my family. Without their encouragement, support and understanding this book could never have been written.

March 1991   Emil J. Kirchner

Abbreviations

CAP	Common Agricultural Policy
COREPER	Committees of Permanent Representatives
CSCE	Conference on Security and Co-operation in Europe
EC	European Community(ies)
ECB	European Central Bank
ECOFIN	Economic and Finance(ial) Council of Ministers
ECSC	European Coal and Steel Community
ECU	European Currency Unit
EEC	European Economic Community
EFTA	European Free Trade Association
EMS	European Monetary System
EMU	Economic and Monetary Union
EPC	European Political Co-operation
ERM	Exchange Rate Mechanism
ESC	Economic and Social Committee
ESCB	European System of Central Banks
EP	Euopean Parliament
IGCs	Intergovernmental Conference(s)
IGC-EMU	Intergovernmental Conference on Economic and Monetary Union
IGC-PU	Intergovernmental Conference on Political Union
MEP	Member of the European Parliament
MFA	Multifibre Agreement
SEA	Single European Act
WEU	Western European Union

1

EC decision-making and co-operative federalism

Introduction

During the first fifteen years of the European Community (EC) there was an overriding emphasis in the literature on the central institutions and political integration.[1] The concept of 'functional or sectoral spillover', the assumption of a zero-sum transfer of competences from national to Community institutions, and the supremacy of Community law were the lifeblood of that literature. It was a combination of economic factors and enlargement in the mid-1970s which reversed the orientation and resulted in studies with a heavy emphasis on national actors in EC decision-making. Though overemphasising the intergovernmental method (in order to attack or erode established beliefs and assumptions), this new school, reflecting realism as its main orientation, introduced a much needed balance to the study of integration and certainly appeared to capture EC developments more closely than earlier concepts had been able to do.[2] However, whilst the intergovernmental method appeared particularly suitable to describe EC decision-making and developments in the 1970s and early 1980s, it seemed to have lost some of its explanatory powers with the arrival of the Single European Act (SEA) in 1986. The widening and deepening of EC institutional competences, and the increasing use of majority voting in the Council of Ministers seemed to give a spur to the integrationists[3] and supranationalists. Yet, the SEA seemed also to give heart to the intergovernmentalists by maintaining the veto, by establishing national safeguards, and by limiting the Commission's implementation powers. The outcome of negotiations for two new treaties on EMU and Political Union in 1991 was viewed with similar assumptions by each school. A central question in the debate between the integrationist and the intergovernmental/realist school is whether the EC will undermine or strengthen the powers of the member states. The intergovernmentalist/realist school argues that member states, far from losing power to Community institutions, as assumed by neo-functionalists, have used the Community framework as an instrument to enhance their interests.[4]

Governments have for a long time played a preponderant role in EC decision-making through the Council of Ministers and the European Council. The Rome Treaty gives the Council of Ministers the power to decide over Commission proposals and to determine the extent of EC collaborative actions. De Gaulle's showdown with the Commission in the 1960s further strengthened the role of the Council. To maintain this privileged position, whilst at the same time trying to preserve a limited 'separation of powers principle' with the Commission and the EP, the Council enlarged its structure in the 1970s. By doing so, it tried to meet pressing problems emanating from the prolonged economic recession, EC enlargement, and international competition. Manifestations of this growing Council structure are, the evolving role of the COREPER (French abbreviation for the Committee of Permanent Representatives), the emergence of 'technical' council of Ministers, the succession of summits by European Councils, the expansion of the General Secretariat of the Council, the upgrading of the Council Presidency, and the strengthening of the Council-controlled implementation procedure of EC legislation, through the insistence on 'Regulatory Committees'.[5]

Not surprisingly the roles of the European Council and the Council Presidency are interlinked.[6] Both operated largely without existing Treaty provisions (until 1986), and both reflected a strengthening of the national component of EC decision-making: signifying that EC decision-making was not characterised by a transfer of powers from the national to the EC level in a zero-sum fashion, but rather by a 'pooling of sovereignties' among member governments in certain policy areas analogous to intergovernmentalist methods.

The arrival of the SEA in 1986 represented the first far-reaching attempt by the EC to amend and extend the Rome Treaties of 1958. It comprised important EC policy, institutional and decision-making changes. Besides the formal introduction of majority voting (in certain areas) in EC decision-making, the SEA has paved the way for co-decisional powers of the EP, through the co-operation and assent procedure, and for a more influential Commission role in EC policy making. It legitimises the work of both the European Council and the Council Presidency and strengthens the role of the Commission. The completion of the internal market by 1992 takes central place in the SEA but there are also other provisions concerning such fields as environmental, monetary and security matters. The latter is particularly interesting, since even realists, like Stanley Hoffmann, admit that should the EC develop a common security policy, the strength of the nation state could be undermined. The SEA and its implementation potential thus reopened the debate about the inevitability of EC integration, or the survival of the nation state. This debate was intensified with the preparations for and start of, negotiations for the two new treaties on EMU and Political Union in 1991.

The role played by the Council Presidency in the implementation of the SEA, and thus by implication in EC decison-making and EC integration, seems to be central. On the one hand, a Council Presidency which is determined to expand upon existing SEA provisions could pave the way towards further EC integration. On the other hand, a Council Presidency which seeks to restrict the application of SEA provisions might help to buttress the interests of the nation states. The interrelationship between the Council Presidency and the implementation of the SEA deserves, therefore, careful attention.

In spite of its apparent importance in EC decision-making, the Council Presidency has only received scant attention in academic literature, and, as far as literature is available, it is directed primarily towards the administrative role[7] rather than the authority of the Presidency. What is needed is systematic study of the way the Council Presidency carries out its work, the conditions which affect its work, and the influence it has on EC integration. A main aim of this book will be to assess the impact of the Council Presidency in EC decision-making and integration. Attention will focus on those eight Council Presidencies which have held terms of office between the beginning of 1986 and the end of 1989. This period coincides with the signing of the SEA in February 1986, its formal adoption in July 1987 and two and a half years of implementation. This period also marks the arrival of Portugal and Spain as new Community members and the regime changes in Eastern Europe. In chronological order these are the Netherlands, the United Kingdom, Belgium, Denmark, the Federal Republic of Germany, Greece, Spain and France. The sample of eight is reasonably well balanced in size (four are large and four are small countries), in length of EC membership (four are founding members, two joined in 1973, one in 1981 and one in 1986), and in outlook (pro-integrationist tendencies are usually associated with the founding members, plus Spain, whilst a certain reluctance towards EC integration is noted with regard to the remaining three countries). These eight presidencies comprise two-thirds of the twelve EC member states.

The empirical part of the study includes a series of interviews with government officials of the respective eight Presidencies; officials of the General Secretariats of the Council of Ministers, the Commission and the EP; and officials of the Secretariat dealing with European Political Co-operation (EPC).[8]

The Commission proposes and the Council disposes?

The Rome Treaties foresaw a sharing in executive powers between the Commission and the Council of Ministers based on the Commission's right to initiate legislation and on the Council of Ministers' obligation to amend Commission proposals only by a unanimous vote. This sharing of executive power has undergone substantial changes since its conception, affecting each institution in relationship to each other and collectively vis-à-vis the EP. On the Commission's side, the French-inspired EC constitutional crisis of 1965 manoeuvred it from a position of executive power-sharing and independence to one which was largely subservient to the Council of Ministers. Yet even in those dark days of Commission history (1966 to 1985) the Commission retained certain executive powers; for example, in the fixing of agricultural prices, external trade policy, competition policy, and coal and steel policy.[9] In addition, the so-called Continental Can Judgment, of the early 1970s, had opened the way for the Commission to exercise some control over the merger of firms within the EC.[10]

Like the Commission, the status of the Council of Ministers has changed over time, both in a horizontal and a vertical direction. Horizontal changes were marked by the arrival of Technical or Specialised Councils (such as those for Agriculture, Social Affairs, European Political Cooperation, the Internal Market, etc.). Vertical change came from a two-fold development. Below the Council of Ministers, a sub-structure emerged in which COREPER, the EPC Political Committee, Specialised Agricultural Committees, the

Committee serving the Council of Ministers dealing with economic and financial affairs (ECOFIN), and the General Secretariat of the Council became increasingly involved in EC decision-making. Above the Council of Ministers, the Heads of State and Government began, from 1969 onward, to play a leading role in Community affairs; initially in the form of infrequent summit meetings and from 1975 onward through the establishment of regularised European Councils. Concomitant with these two expansions came an augmentation in the role of the Council Presidency, which, with only a modest treaty base, has, since 1966, developed pragmatically and incrementally.[11]

The Council Presidency's functions comprise administration, initiation, mediation, representation and implementation. They involve: administrative tasks in the co-ordination of meetings at various Council levels; the initiation of EPC matters; the attempt to mediate and to find compromise solutions among its partners and between the Council and the Commission or EP; the representation of Council positions both with regard to other EC institutions, and with regard to third countries; and the implementation of EPC decisions. The Presidency shares with the Commission functions concerning the initiation, representation and implementation of policies. It is thus important in terms of agenda-setting, consensus-building and collective representation. The roles of the Presidency and the Commission are both collaborative and conflictual. The Commission, as the guardian of the treaties and the initiator of policy, shares with the Presidency the desire to see agreement on the proposals under discussion; but while the Commission wishes to see its version adopted, the Presidency has to make an assessment of what the twelve member states will accept. While in some circumstances the Commission can be overruled unanimously by the Council, it must give its agreement to any amended proposal before it can be adopted. This arrangement is at the heart of the Community's decision-making procedure, as the Council can seldom achieve unanimity to overrule the Commission. In circumstances where qualified majority voting applies the Presidency will try to get the necessary qualified majority but always with an eye on the Commission proposal.[12] However, both the Commission and the Council Presidency have a mobilising effect on EC decision-making.

It is this sharing of functions and competences between the EC institutions and national governments which symbolises the very essence of the EC, but which also demonstrates the complexity of the integration process.[13] Clearly, there is a strong element of national control in the process of integration which allows the pooling of sovereignties in certain fields but ensures that there is not a zero-sum transfer of competences from the national to the Community context. In other words, the aim is to engage in trade-offs on sovereignty; what might be lost individually can be gained collectively through a common stand or policy. The preference is, therefore, to maintain the intergovernmental method as far as possible and for national governments to act, wherever possible, as gatekeepers between domestic political systems and the Community. The European Council fulfils this purpose reasonably well in that it helps to serve the national interest of the member states. At the same time, the European Council is a mirror of the EC inability to move from negotiation (in which each member state defends or promotes its own national interest in a zero-sum fashion) to collective problem-solving.[14] The decision-making system of the EC is thus dependent on the member states reaching agreement.

With the specialisation and expansion of the Council structure a number of consequences occurred of which two deserve a mention. Firstly, it became more difficult to locate the centre of power in EC decision-making. Some decisions could be taken at COREPER level, particularly on so-called A Points[15]; others were passed at European Council level.[16] This expanded the number of key actors involved but also made decision-making more cumbersome. Matters were often passed between the Council of Ministers and the European Council, where the latter finally arbitrated on them. Some observers have seen this as undermining the Council of Ministers' credibility and turning the Council of Ministers into a secretariat incapable of making decisions autonomously.[17] However, decision-making at the European Council level opened the way for participation of the top national decision-makers and for package deals which enlarged the EC decision-making capacities. It also promoted the launching of major policy initiatives. In all this, though the Commission continued (and continues) to propose and the Council of Ministers to dispose, the authenticity of both the 'proposer' and the 'disposer' became blurred. Often either the Council of Ministers or the European Council provides the Commission with a mandate to propose Community policy, and often decisions are informally adopted either below or above the Council of Ministers' level. In addition, there are situations, as in competition policy, where the Commission itself takes decisions which are binding. Moreover, since 1975 the EP is empowered to adopt the EC budget.

Secondly, despite the EP's right to adopt the EC budget, the dominant role exercised by either the European Council or the Council of Ministers in EC decision-making has kept EP powers to a minimum. The Council of Ministers and its members combine the roles of negotiators and legislators.[18] In addition, the right to initiate legislation rests with the Commission rather than with the EP. The culmination of these constraints is seen as representing a 'demo-cratic deficit' in EC decision-making. (See below for further details.) Equally, the Council sub-structure parallels that of the Commission and thus challenges the Commission's role. As each endeavours to assert its role, there is considerable tension between the Presidency, which in this context is the representation of the Council, the Com-mission and the European Parliament.[19] However, as Helen Wallace points out, the office of the Presidency embodies both con-tradictions, in the task of 'pushing and hauling', and temptations to 'play the role of proxy Prime Minister or President'.[20]

The Council Presidency, the SEA and integration approaches

The six-monthly Council Presidency presents both opportunities and challenges. It offers opportunities to launch desired policy priorities but also offers challenges to obtain the necessary support from the other partners in achieving those priorities. A Presidency has to set its objectives, organise the necessary resources, and plan its activity in order to achieve those objectives. However, the agenda is largely predetermined because Community work is a continuum, not a stop-go process linked to particular Presidencies. The Council Presidency acts as a catalyst or consensus former. This mediation function is enhanced depending on the size of the country in ques-tion, its economic or political weight, or its diplomatic skill, innovativeness, bureaucratic experience, and timing. The European Council, because of its high-level participants, represents an impor-tant vehicle through which the Presidency carries out its mediation function. Close and effective collaboration is required with the Com-mission, which formally holds the right to initiate Community policy and legislation. Undoubtedly, favourable economic and political conditions are of importance; periods of economic prosperity, for example, are more conducive to co-operation than periods of economic recession; countries are more receptive to compromises after a general election than before. Thus, different conditions, skills and issues need careful analysis in assessing the effect of a given Presidency. To narrow the problems generally associated with the assessment of impact, this research will confine itself largely to the contribution which different Presidencies have made towards the implementation of the SEA. In other words, the SEA will be used as a yardstick for measuring the impact of the Presidency. Considering the role the Council Presidency has assumed in EC decision-making, it is reasonable to suggest that this role will be of great importance for the extent to which the SEA will be implemented.

The SEA entailed an expansion of Community policies, a strengthening of the EC institutional competences, and a more effective decision-making procedure. Stark differences prevailed during the negotiations over how these three components could be combined, and the end product represented a compromise among the different views held by the EC member states. The compromise reached by the end of 1985 was the outcome of a number of attempts, dating back to the early 1970s to revise the Rome Treaties or to establish new Treaties. Milestones in this sequence were the call for a Political Union at the 1972 Paris Summit, the 1975 Report on European Union (known as the Tindemans' Report), the 1979 Report on the European Institutions (known as the Report of the Three Wise Men), the Solemn Declaration of the 1983 Stuttgart Summit, the 1984 EP Draft Treaty on Political Union, and the 1985 Report of the Ad Hoc Committee for Institutional Affairs (known as the Dooge Report).

The SEA represents a platform through which the Presidency can achieve measurable and meaningful results. However, both the content and the means to achieve the SEA's stipulated aims were, and are, contested. Some EC member states appear satisfied with a mere de-regulation exercise of the internal market programme, whilst others prefer to add common policies in the monetary, fiscal, environmental and social fields to the liberalisation of market restrictions. This poses the following questions. Can the SEA be seen as a springboard for European integration? Integration, at the political level, can be described as the process by which larger political units either solely or jointly with national administrations conduct the business now carried out by national governments.[21] Alternatively, was the SEA indicative of a trend whereby national governments preserve or increase their prerogatives? The progression of the EC treaties since 1951, although gradual, seems to be indicative of the neo-functional logic of 'spillover'.[22] On the other hand, the SEA contains 'escape' clauses, which appear to safeguard prerogatives and which are not found as extensively in the original EC Treaty. Safeguards of this sort are not characteristic of integrative efforts, as viewed by the neo-functionalist school, and might be better understood through the concept of international regimes, defined by Krasner as networks of rules, norms and procedures which regularise international behaviour and control its effects.[23]

The implementation of the SEA thus represents an important test of the work of the Council Presidency. It will help to show whether the Presidency was being used as an instrument to safeguard and promote national interests rather than as a mechanism to foster co-operation or to enhance Community integration. If, for example, more of the former can be detected we may find the impact of the Presidency associated with a disjointed trend of SEA accomplishments rather than an accumulative one; a disruptive influence on the medium-to-long term goals of EC integration. It is against this background that an examination of the Presidency's influence in the implementation of the SEA should help in the task of analysing the progress and direction of EC integration; of establishing whether the SEA is seen more as an end in itself than as a springboard for further integration; and of clarifying whether the realist school will continue to be more appropriate in explaining the phenomenon of EC integration than the neo-functionalist one.

Joseph Weiler has identified two dynamics of integration: (1) a judicial–normative dynamic with an emphasis on treaty provisions and, ultimately, judicial review by the Court; and (2) a political decisional dynamic, characterised by incrementalism and package dealing in the policy-making framework.[24] The SEA has helped to stimulate both dynamics. The SEA established a number of important provisions in policy and institutional terms, especially as they relate to the completion of the internal market and the inter-institutional relations. However, there were important limits in a judicial sense in that , for example, EPC was left outside the Community legal framework, and the 1992 deadline for the internal market was not legally binding.[25] The 1987 Delors package is an example of how important the political decisional dynamic can be in the areas of agricultural and budgetary reforms, as well as financial aid for the under-developed regions. The same dynamic can be observed with regard to the establishment and proceedings of the Delors Committee on Economic and Monetary Union (1988–89). It is this second dynamic, therefore, which deserves major attention. Though the Commission is an important actor in the policy-making framework, it is at the various Council levels (COREPER, Council of Ministers, and the European Council) where the pace and extent of this policy-making is being determined. The Council Presidency is a key actor at all decision-making levels.

The concept of co-operative federalism

Who decides what, when and how is a crucial determinant in any decision-making process; involving questions of scope, competence, effectiveness, fairness and accountability. EC decision-making is no exception, but more complex than national decision-making. This has to do with the limited treaty base, the allocation of competences among the various institutions, the forms of co-operation (inter-governmentalism versus the Community method), and the voting methods (unanimity versus majority). In certain fields like coal, steel, CAP, commercial trade, competition policy, and the internal market, where treaty provisions prevail, the Community pursues common policies, often by majority voting procedures, which can be enforced or changed by judgments of the Court of Justice. In other areas, member states co-operate without a treaty base, through established conventions such as those for monetary policy, cultural policy and EPC; these require unanimity. Whereas the former expands Community competences and gradually erodes national sovereignty, the latter tends to maintain national interests and sovereignty. However, the intergovernmentalist method can also regularise and routinise matters sufficiently to act as a springboard for the establishment of Community methods. In other words, the informal practice becomes formal or legitimised through proper Community procedures. The SEA is a prime example of this.

The European policy-making system is marked by economic, cultural and political interdependence which transcends borders and penetrates deeply into the national realms.[26] Yet it was not until the mid-1980s that scholars began to examine the relationship between national and Community policies.[27] In subsequent studies, the importance of a mixed national/Community system emerged in which the emphasis was placed on the 'pooling of sovereignties' and co-operative federalism. This mix of national and Community competences can, of course, already be found in Monnet's and Schuman's idea to pool national sovereignties in areas of strategic importance for the creation of war industries.[28] The term co-operative federalism implies the 'pooling' and -mixing- of national sovereignty with Community powers and serves as a policy-making model between the national and the Community level.[29] It is derived from the experience of federal systems, especially that of the Federal Republic of Germany, which changed from a dualistically conceived federal state to co-operative federalism.[30] The emergent 'joint tasks' in the West German federal structure have been characterised by Fritz Scharpf as *Politikverflechtung* whereby the responsible bodies of the federation and the *Laender* make use of a commonly determined authority, e.g. planning, decision-making, financing and, to some extent, administration. These commonly planned and financed tasks are concerned with economic and structural matters of national importance that require heavy investments in infrastructure by the *Laender* and municipalities. It signifies a situation whereby the federal and *Laend* governments hardly make policy decisions alone anymore.[31] This phenomenon applies to other countries as well. As Lucio Levi points out, a growing number of political objectives require the co-ordinated intervention of both levels of government and a joint commitment to accomplish them.[32] Co-operative federalism thus marks a shift from a distribution of powers between the two levels of government (which reflects the previous criterion of exclusive jurisdiction) to a model based on concurrent jurisdiction.

Bulmer and Wessels suggest that the tendency to overstep the vertical separation of power in the EC stems from the tasks of modern welfare states in an interdependent world. They therefore argue that the evolution of the EC into a system of co-operative federalism results from a dilemma:

On the one hand, governments see the need to enlarge the scope of EC activities in order better to fulfil the needs of national welfare states, on the other, they are reluctant to give up control over their policies. As a result of this governments and national bureaucracies are in a permanent process of 'transnational' negotiation.[33]

According to Bulmer and Wessels each participating level of government must be prepared to engage in some shared problem solving, whether in the specific context of the EC's competences or in a looser framework of mutual adjustment between the policies of the national governments. The European Council is the key forum for both sorts of engagements. The European Council helps to pool the responsibilities and resources of both the national and EC level of governments. It is a means whereby the Heads of State and Government can address the sovereignty versus interdependence dilemma by co-operative means.[34]

Putnam's two-level game analysis is helpful here. He characterises international negotiations as the interplay between a game at the national and international level. At the national level, 'domestic groups seek to maximise their interests by pressuring the government to adopt favourable policies, and politicians seek power by constructing coalitions among these groups'. At the international level, 'national governments seek to maximise their own freedom to satisfy domestic pressures, while minimising the adverse consequences of foreign developments'. Accordingly:

these two games are played simultaneously, so that national policies are in some sense the resultant of both the domestic and the international parallelogram of forces. Neither of the two games can be ignored by policy-makers, so long as their countries remain interdependent, yet sovereign democracies. A national political leader appears at both game boards.[35]

In the EC context, influence is exerted both ways: domestic considerations influence co-operation at the European level, while decisions in the European Council often transcend into the national context. As Hoscheit points out, in their negotiations in the European Council, the Heads of Government must integrate into their strategic and tactical calculation a number of purely domestic factors which they, as supreme representatives of their national political systems, cannot choose to ignore. Among these factors, constitutional rules play a role in certain countries.[36]

Co-operative federalism thus signifies situations in which national governments and supranational institutions engage to an advanced degree in joint tasks, joint sharing of competences and responsibilities, and problem solving exercises. The progression or evolution between intergovernmentalism, which is characteristic of the activities of most international organisations, and co-operative federalism, which typifies the EC, is depicted in the decision-making typology set out in Table 1.1. This table, which has been modelled after the framework presented by Ernst Haas,[37] highlights the different modes of decision-making between low and high levels of integration at the institutional level.

Table 1.1 *Types of decision-making*

	Decision-making style	Voting method	Degree to which joint action is carried out	Type of interaction
Low	Lowest common denominator	Mostly unanimity	Co-ordination	Inter-govern-mentalism
	Splitting the difference	Some majority voting	Co-operation	Hybrid between Inter-govern-mentalism and Co-operative federalism
High	Upgrading the common interest	Mostly majority voting	Problem solving	Co-operative federalism

Low levels of integration describe situations in which member states try to harmonise their different prevailing national interests. They attempt to co-ordinate their disparate views and to adopt a decision according to the lowest common denominator by ensuring that no country is asked to make any substantial sacrifices. Since decisions are unanimous in such situations, each issue is treated individually rather than connected with other issues in a package deal formula. This form of decision-making gives governments a preponderant amount of influence in decision-making, curtails the role of the Commission and the EP, and amounts to inter-governmentalism. Member states are reluctant to do things jointly, and have limited trust in their partners to abide by common policy agreements.

Whereas co-ordination implies a harmonious relationship, a minimising of sacrifices and a slow pace of integration (dictated by the slowest mover in the convoy), co-operation entails trade-offs, negotiation and a certain amount of conflict over how benefits can be jointly shared. The emphasis is on joint efforts of operation and is connected with growing economic, social or political inter-dependence among states. Co-operation thus signifies the existence of some majority voting, which allows member states to split their differences rather than go on co-ordinating until the lowest common denominator has been reached. Both the Commission and the EP hold certain, though limited, competences and engage in joint efforts with national governments over Community policies. Though inter-governmental methods are still practised, as the number of joint tasks increases, the intergovernmental method impedes the extent to which co-operative federalism can be practised.

Co-operative federalism signifies the existence of joint tasks between national governments and Community institutions, the widespread practice of majority voting, and an orientation towards problem solving rather than the splitting of differences, which often allows only sub-optimal outcome in policy making.[38] Governments remain the vehicle of integration but engage to a considerable degree in the sharing of competences with Community institutions.

However, whilst the Community appears to adopt increasingly co-operative federalist methods, it is important to point out the likely side-effects. Co-operative federalism co-exists with a tendency towards centralisation.[39] Moreover, in the German context, from which the principle predominantly originated, there are indications that the system is engendering high administrative costs, a bureaucratisation of the decision-making process, and an exclusion of (*Laend*) parliaments from the decision-making process. Problems have also arisen in Germany as a result of an opaque decision-making process and a diffusion of responsibility due to joint poli-cies.[40] Therefore, without adequate provisions to the contrary, the prevailing 'democratic deficit' in EC decision-making would prob-ably continue under the system of co-operative federalism.

The democratic deficit

The democratic deficit refers to those areas of EC activity which are not directly held accountable by elected representatives, whether in national parliaments or the EP.[41] To a large extent this is derived from the fact that the Council of Ministers, rather than the EP, acts as the legislative branch of the EC, and that both the Council of Ministers and the European Council meet in secret; hiding the details and alliances which are made in the adoption or delay of decisions. Although the EP has the right to censure the Commission, it has no right to dispose over the Council of Ministers. And even its power of censure over the Commission can be compared with equipping a traffic warden with a nuclear bomb. Because of its blanket nature (only the entire Commission can be dismissed), it has been used very

rarely. There is also no decisive role for the EP in the investiture of a
new Commission.

The question can be raised of whether the Council of Ministers or
the European Council meetings should be made more accountable to
national parliaments, as already practised by the Danish parliament.[42] This could be supplemented or reinforced through the establishment of a second chamber/senate.[43] Other suggestions involve a
stronger link between national parliaments and the EP. However, if
practised on a large scale, such a link might disrupt existing national
legislative–executive relations. On the other hand, national parliaments which have been cut off from policy-making may see this as an
opportunity to increase their own power vis-à-vis the national
executive.[44] There is also the question of whether, and if so to what
extent, subnational governments or parliaments should be involved
or consulted in EC decision-making. Already, the German *Laender*,
which have substantial prerogatives in the cultural, educational and
environmental domain, feel increasingly affected by Community
decisions. As the Community moves further into areas such as
training, broadcasting and environmental protection, subnational
governments and parliaments may try to further institutionalise their
access to Community institutions. In response to the SEA, the
Bundesrat (the German upper house which represents the state
governments) has already sought greater access to German federal
government negotiations in EC affairs.[45]

Aims and structure

This book focuses on the EC decision-making process and seeks to
assess the relative strength and influence of the actors involved.
Stress is placed on the Council Presidency and on the empirical question of whether the Council Presidency is primarily a tool to defend
and promote national interest rather than Community interest.
Insights into the power distribution among EC institutions and
between the national and the Community level will hopefully tell
us something about the future of the nation state and the relevance of
competing approaches to the study of integration. The aims of the
book fall into four categories.

1   A critical review of existing approaches to the study of
    integration and an attempt to assess their relevance for explain-

ing the motives for, and content of, the SEA and the linkage
between the SEA and the two Intergovernmental Conferences on
EMU (IGC-EMU) and on Political Union (IGC-PU).
2   An examination of the reasons for, and the substance of, the SEA,
    e.g. what were the forces and actors responsible for the SEA and
    what are its main policy and institutional innovations.
3   A comparative analysis of the role of the Council Presidency and
    an assessment of the impact of the Presidency in the implementa-
    tion of the SEA and the preparation of the IGC-EMU and
    IGC-PU.
4   An evaluation of the factors leading to the IGC-EMU and
    IGC-PU, the negotiation-setting of these two Intergovernmental
    Conferences, the developments of EC decision-making, and the
    relationship between national governments and EC institutions.

Now follows a summary of subsequent chapters. Chapter 2 reviews
a number of competing theoretical orientations in the study of
European integration and seeks to determine which theoretical
approach appears most relevant in explaining EC developments.
Special consideration is given to the SEA and the two Intergovernmental Conferences on EMU and Political Union.

Why the SEA came into being when it did and in the form it did is
the subject of investigation in chapter 3. The chapter will make an
assessment of what the SEA represents in the process of integration,
and the challenges it poses in implemention; can implementation, for
example, help to establish EC macro-economic policies? Whether
the SEA has contributed to more democracy in EC decision-making
will be another investigative question of the chapter. And if this is the
case has it occurred at the expense of efficiency in the EC decision-
making process? (i.e. will the 'two-reading procedure' and the qualified majority required in the EP to amend the Council of Ministers'
'common position' disrupt and delay EC decision-making?). How
does the Commission deal with the two-fold pressure of not wanting
to upset either the Council or the EP? Why is there an apparent
problem over the implementation procedures of Acts adopted by the
Council; i.e. why does the Council insist on being involved in implementation and why can the Commission not carry out its task as
assigned by the treaty?

Chapter 4 examines the segmented Council structure (European
Council, Council of Ministers, COREPER, Secretariats, and Com-

mittees) and the role of the Presidency. It will dwell principally on how the Presidency functions, the context in which it works and the tasks it performs rather than on what effect it has had. It will also explore when and why the Council Presidency assumed such an important role in EC decision-making.

Chapter 5 sets the stage for assessing the opportunities and challenges faced by Council Presidencies. The major achievements of the SEA between 1986 and 1989 will be used as a yardstick for measuring the impact of the Council Presidency in EC decision-making and integration. The aim is to determine whether the Presidency contributed to an expansive rather than a restrictive implementation of the SEA. The chapter will explore how the Presidency is involved in the agenda-setting for EC policies, the stance it takes towards integration (favourable or reluctant), and the conditions which affect the role of the Presidency. Under the latter, consideration will be given to the tasks inherited from the previous Presidency, the type of leadership provided in achieving compromise or consensus in Council decisions, and the extent to which co-operation was attempted, or obtained, with the Commission and the EP. Other points of detail involve an examination of the prevailing economic and political climate under which the eight Presidencies have operated, i.e. prosperity versus recession, or pre-election periods versus post-election periods. Attention will also be paid to the size of the country holding the Presidency; do 'small' countries, for example, have advantages over large ones or vice-versa? The chapter also considers the means by which compromises were achieved internally and positions successfully defended vis-à-vis the Commission and the EP. Another focus of the chapter will be to analyse the different styles in which Presidencies carry out their role; are they innovative, conventional or crisis-management oriented? Finally, we examine whether and how the role of the Presidency in EC decision-making could or should be improved.

Chapter 6 will analyse the factors which brought about the IGC-EMU and IGC-PU, the process of negotiation over the content of the two new treaties, the relevance of the principle of subsidiarity, and the implications of these developments for the future of the EC and the nation state. This assessment will also relate to the distribution of power among the Commission, the Council of Ministers and the European Parliament. Is there now a more equal power distribution among the three institutions than prior to 1986? Has power really shifted away from the Council of Ministers? Another point of interest will be to evaluate two mainstream theories, realism and neo-functionalism, in the light of both the empirical evidence gathered on the authority of the Presidency and developments surrounding the IGC-EMU and the IGC-PU. The chapter will finish with an assessment of one of the main points of the book, namely, the relationship or co-existence between the EC and the national states. What signs are there that the former is undermining the powers of the latter?

Conclusion

The EC is characterised by a sharing of functions and competences between the EC institutions and national governments. There is a strong element of national control in the process of EC decision-making which allows the pooling of sovereignties in certain fields but ensures that there is not a zero-sum transfer of competences from the national to the Community context. Governments act as gatekeepers between domestic political systems and the Community wherever possible. Whilst this helps to serve the national interest of the member states, it impedes the EC moving from negotiation to collective problem-solving. Decisions in the EC resemble partly inter-governmental and partly co-operative federal practices. Governments increasingly need to engage in transnational activities to meet domestic demands and they feel the constraints of growing social and political interdependence as well as the effect of common EC policies. Nevertheless, as far as possible, they try to secure national control. This is visible in the aims and implementation procedures of the SEA and is surfacing in the IGC-EMU and the IGC-PU in the shape of the subsidiarity principle, according to which, policies should be formulated at the lowest possible level of government.

The Council Presidency is at the interface of national and Community competences and assumes great importance in the way national interest will be defended and Community interest will be promoted. It plays a crucial role in the agenda-setting of the various levels of Council (European Council, Council of Ministers and COREPER) and acts as a catalyst or consensus former in EC decision-making. Establishing whether the Council Presidency contributed to an expansive, rather than a restrictive, implementation of the SEA will therefore help to shed light on whether the role of the

Council Presidency can be seen more as a vehicle to defend national interest than as a tool to promote Community interest. Insights into the impact of the Council Presidency, the power distribution among EC institutions (including trade-offs between decision-making efficiency and democratic control) and between the national and the Community level will hopefully tell us something about the future of the nation state and the relevance of competing approaches to the study of integration. It is to the relevance of theoretical approaches that Chapter 2 will turn.

Notes

1 This was evident, for example, in the titles and content of the following books. Ernst B. Haas, *The Uniting of Europe; Political, Social, and Economic Forces, 1950–1957*, Stanford, 1958; David Mitrany, *A Working Peace System*, Chicago, 1966; Leon Lindberg and Stuart Scheingold, *Europe's Would-be Polity*, Englewood Cliffs, 1970; Joseph Nye, *Peace in Parts: Integration and Conflict in Regional Organisation*, Boston, 1971; and Leon Lindberg and Stuart Scheingold, eds, *Regional Integration: Theory and Research*, Cambridge, 1971.

2 Among the most conspicuous voices were: Helen Wallace, William Wallace and Carole Webb, eds, *Policy Making in the European Communities*, Chichester, 1978; and Paul Taylor, *The Limits of European Integration*, London, 1983.

3 For a thorough analysis of the theoretical relevance of different approaches to an understanding of the causes and implications of the SEA see Andrew Moravcsik, 'Negotiating the Single European Act: National Interests and Conventional Statecraft in the European Community', *International Organization*, XLV, 1, 1991, pp. 19–56.

4 This point is made most strongly by Alan Milward, *The Reconstruction of Western Europe 1945–1951*, London, 1987.

5 For further details see, for example, Gianni Bonvicini and Elfriede Regelsberger, 'The Decision-making Process in the EC's European Council', *The International Spectator*, XXII, 3, 1987, pp. 152–75; and Simon Bulmer and Wolfgang Wessels, *The European Council: Decision-making in European Politics*, London, 1987.

6 This is particularly well illustrated in Guy de Bassompierre, *Changing the Guard in Brussels: An Insider's View of the EC Presidency*, New York, 1988.

7 See, for example, Colm O Nuallain, ed., with the collaboration Jean-Marc Hoscheit, *The Presidency of the European Council of Ministers. Impacts and Implications for National Governments*, London, 1985.

8 Around fifty officials were interviewed; about five from each of the eight Presidencies examined, with at least one dealing with EPC matters, and about three officials each from the Commission, the General Secretariat of the Council of Ministers, the General Secretariat of the European Parlia-

ment, and the EPC Secretariat. Usually, a four page outline of the themes and questions to be raised in the interview was submitted in advance.

9   In 1977 Article 58 of the ECSC Treaty was invoked by a Council decision which empowered the Commission to establish a Community-wide system of production quotas in steel.

10   For details see the analysis provided by Willy Alexander, *Common Market Law Review*, X, 1973, pp. 311–19.

11   For details on the development of the Council Presidency see Annette Morgan, 'From summit to council: evolution in the EC', Political and Economic Planning, European Series no. 27, June 1976; Helen Wallace and Geoffrey Edwards, 'European Community: the evolving role of the Presidency of the Council', *International Affairs*, October 1976, pp. 535–50; O Nuallain, ed., with Hoscheit, 'The Presidency of the European Council of Ministers'; and de Bassompierre, *Changing the Guard in Brussels*.

12   See Denis O'Leary, 'The Irish Presidency of the European Community', paper delivered at the UACES and Irish Association for Contemporary European Studies, Kings College, London, 24 October 1990, p. 6.

13   See de Bassompierre, *Changing the Guard in Brussels*, pp. 121–3; and Jean-Marc Hoscheit, 'The European Council and domestic policy making', Jean-Marc Hoscheit and Wolfgang Wessels, *The European Council 1974–1986: Evaluation and Prospects*, Maastricht, 1988, pp. 61–104.

14   See Fritz Scharpf, 'The joint-decision trap: lessons from German federalism and European integration', *Public Administration*, autumn 1988, pp. 239–78. On the implications of the European Council see Bulmer and Wessels, *The European Council*.

15   'A' points are those on which COREPER has found that there is agreement and Council discussion is not required. 'A' points are formally approved in Council meetings. 'B' points are those which require ministerial discussion. For further details see William Nicoll and Trevor C. Salmon, *Understanding the European Communities*, London, 1990, p. 60.

16   Conclusions of the European Council are not legal acts, even though in some cases the decisions made in the European Council have been so detailed that they could be transformed directly into Community regulations without any further change. For further details see Bonvicini and Regelsberger, 'The Decision-making Process in the EC's European Council', p. 162.

17   Ibid., pp. 169–70.

18   For an excellent treatment of the role of the Council of Ministers see Helen Wallace, 'The Presidency of the Council of Ministers of the European Community: task and evolution', in O Nuallain, ed., with Hoscheit, *The Presidency of the European Council of Ministers*, pp. 1–22.

19   See O'Leary, 'The Irish Presidency of the European Community', p. 5.

20   Wallace, 'The Presidency: task and evolution', p. 2

21   This definition is derived from Walter S. Jones, *The Logic of International Relations*, 6th edition, Boston, 1988, p. 622. For a more elaborate analysis of definitions of European integration see William Wallace, *The*

Transformation of Western Europe, London, 1990, especially chapter 4.

22   For further details, see Haas, *The Uniting of Europe*; Ernst B. Haas, *Beyond the Nation-State: Functionalism and International Organization*, Stanford, 1964; and Ernst B. Haas, 'The uniting of Europe and the uniting of Latin America', *Journal of Common Market Studies*, V, 1967, pp. 315–43.

23   Stephen Krasner, ed., *International Regimes*, Ithaca, 1983.

24   Joseph Weiler, 'Community, member states and European integration: is the law relevant?', *Journal of Common Market Studies*, XXI, 1982, pp. 39–56.

25   The end of 1992 deadline does not create an automatic legal effect as regards the free circulation of goods, capital, services and people, nor upon the Council of Ministers to adopt the necessary legislation. But where the Council of Ministers has decided, member states are still required to adapt their national legislation within the deadlines laid down in each directive. Where they fail to do so on time, they can indeed be taken to the Court of Justice. I am grateful to Richard Corbett for clarifying this point to me.

26   Hoscheit, 'The European Council and domestic policy making', p. 100.

27   See Simon Bulmer, *The Domestic Structure of European Community Policy-Making in West Germany*, New York, 1986.

28   Reinhardt Rummel, 'Testing regional integration: new challenges for the Community's foreign policy', unpublished paper, September 1990, p. 9.

29   For details about the origins of the term co-operative federalism see Bulmer and Wessels, The European Council, especially p. 10.

30   For details on German federalism see Arthur B. Gunlicks, ed., 'Federalism and intergovernmental relations in West Germany: a fortieth year appraisal', *Publius*, XIX, 4, fall 1989, especially the chapter by Harmutt Klatt.

31   See Harmutt Klatt, 'Forty years of German federalism: past trend and new developments', in Arthur B. Gunlicks, ed., *Federalism and Intergovernmental Relations in West Germany*, p. 189.

32   Lucio Levi, 'Recent developments in federalist theory', *The Federalist*, 2, 1987, p. 99.

33   Bulmer and Wessels, *The European Council*, pp. 10–11.

34   Hoscheit, 'The European Council and domestic policy making', p. 93.

35   Robert Putnam, 'The Western economic summits: a political interpretation', Cesare Merlini, ed., *Economic Summits and Western Decision-Making*, London, 1984, pp. 48–49

36   Hoscheit, 'The European Council and domestic policy making', pp. 93–4.

37   Ernst B. Haas, 'International integration. The European and the universal process', *International Political Communities*, an anthology, New York, 1966, pp. 93–129.

38   For further details see Scharpf, 'The joint-decision trap'.

39   See Klatt, 'Forty years of German federalism', pp. 185–202. See also Levi, 'Recent developments in federalist theory', pp. 97–136.

40   See Klatt, 'Forty years of German federalism', p. 192.

41 For further details see Shirley Williams, 'Sovereignty and accountability in the European Community', *Political Quarterly*, LXI, 3, 1990, pp. 299–317.

42 For details on the control powers of the Danish parliament (the Folketing) over the Danish government in EC negotiations see John Fitzmaurice, 'The Danish system of parliamentary control over European Community policy', Valentine Herman and Rinus van Schendelen, eds, *The European Parliament and the National Parliaments*, Westmead, 1979, pp. 201–18.

43 See Vernon Bogdanor, *Democratising the Community*, Federal Trust for Education and Research, London, June 1990.

44 See Alberta Sbragia, 'The European Community and institutional development: politics, money, and law', paper prepared for the Brookings Institution's Conference on 'European political institutions and policymaking after 1992', 29–30 March 1990, p. 56.

45 See Rudolf Hrbek, 'The German Laender and the European Community: towards a real federalism?', in Wolfgang Wessels and Elfriede Regelsberger, eds, *The Federal Republic of Germany and the European Community: The Presidency and Beyond*, Bonn, 1988, pp. 215–30.

2

Theoretical endeavours on European integration

Introduction

The 1970s marked a watershed in the theoretical appraisal of European Community (EC) development, especially with regard to the anticipated transfer of decision-making powers from the national to the EC level. Theoretical approaches such as federalism, functionalism, and neo-functionalism,[1] were found wanting in the face of mounting national economic diversity and insufficient EC insulation from international events (monetary, energy and commercial).[2] International relations generally, rather than European affairs, became the focus of attention and was fostered through such concepts as interdependence[3] and international regime.[4] Equally, realism with its emphasis on national autonomy, competition and security, regained credibility.[5] With a weakening of the EC Commission and an expanding Council of Ministers, scholars chose to describe EC activities as intergovernmentalism,[6] highlighting the importance of national interests and interdependence. Economic historians, such as Alan Milward, put the case more strongly when suggesting that the national interest had been the overriding concern in EC co-operation and would continue to be so.[7] In their view, member states have actually used the EC to extend their national interests and have strengthened rather than surrendered their sovereignty. Gradualist integration theory was considered as having become obsolete.[8]

Developments in the 1980s, specially the second half, question the tenor of realist assumptions without, however, restoring sufficient confidence in the validity of gradualist integration. Among these developments are the adoption of the Single European Act (SEA), the first major amendment and expansion of the 1958 Rome Treaties, a strengthening of Franco–German co-operation and changes in East–

West relations. Significantly, the expansion of EC functions via the
SEA coincides with a general growth in the role of individual EC
states[9] and does not, to any significant degree as yet, imply a loss of
sovereignty or legitimacy on the part of EC member states. Stanley
Hoffmanns' prediction that a half-way house between state and EC
jurisdiction could not endure, appears to be inaccurate.[10]

How can this dualism in power-sharing or symbiosis in decision-
making be adequately explained? Do nationalistic behavioural patterns, described in international regime analysis, provide meaningful
guidelines? Or is the EC basically too different from international
organisations (the typical unit of analysis chosen by international
regime scholars) in terms of functions, jurisdictions and resources, to
be assessed comprehensively within such a framework? Alternatively, if comparisons with international organisations are rejected,
can we maintain a rationalistic focus but derive our reference point
from the study of federal systems? Both William Wallace and Fritz
Scharpf, though for different reasons, suggest a federal analogy for
an assessment of the EC.[11] Consistent with such a perspective is the
belief that a close link exists between the development of Western
European states and the functions of the EC system.[12]

To determine the relevance of contesting approaches requires
empirical examination which could centre on; (1) why did EC co-
operation in the shape of the SEA, become a prominent feature in the
1980s, after diversity had been the dominant trend in the 1970s; and
(2) why can we expect that the Council Presidency will play an
important role in how the SEA will be implemented?

Divergence between aspirations and reality

The impact of the Luxembourg compromise of 1966, the EC
enlargement in the early 1970s, international disorder in the monetary and energy field, and the economic crisis, resulted in increasing
diversity and a strengthening of nationalism within the EC. With the
growing politicisation of EC economic activities and the continuing
insistence by national bureaucracies to act as gatekeepers of national
interest, the weaknesses of neo-functionalist explanations were
exposed in the 1970s. The development of the Council of Ministers
and the European Council, and the decline of the Commission, were
yet further signals that neo-functionalism was out of step with EC
developments. It was, therefore, not surprising that Haas's admis-

sion that neo-functionalism had limitations in explaining EC developments[13] undermined interest in integration theory and induced scholars to move to other theoretical pursuits. The decline of neo-functionalism did not mean, however, that theoretical interest in the study of European integration had stopped.

Two different frameworks emerged in the 1970s, one with a realist or intergovernmental perspective and the other based on an international or liberal institutionalist perspective.[14] The former saw integration as reflecting governments' wishes, serving national interests and being controlled by national institutions. In other words, national interests determine the scope and the depth of the integration process, and governments maintain control over the process and over the institutions involved.[15] Far-reaching integration under this framework seems limited given the reluctance of national governments to provide the central institutional means necessary for such integration. Thus national policy-makers, according to this perspective, see the need for establishing economies of scale, in the face of pressing international competitiveness and domestic welfare and service demands, but resist the transfer of controls to central institutions.

Whilst the intergovernmentalist/realist perspective seemed attractive to some scholars such as Stanley Hoffmann, Robert Jordan and Werner Feld,[16] it never became a central focus among scholars for studying the EC, and its credentials seemed to wane further once the Single European Act was signed and ratified. This is not to say that it has become useless, but rather to note that whilst EC developments in the 1970s favourably reflected intergovernmentalist/realist explanations, developments in the 1980s seemed to diverge from this perspective.

If the EC was treated as an appendage of national interest by intergovernmentalist/realists, scholars using interdependence or international regimes as their conceptual tools, were equally scathing about the EC. To Donald Puchala, for example, the EC was at worst a mere international regime or, at best, a system of managed interdependence.[17]

International regimes

One of the dominant schools of thought in the 1980s, especially in the USA was that of international regimes,[18] and various attempts have been made to apply this theoretical orientation to EC behavioural developments.[19] The concept of international regimes comes in a variety of forms. Robert Keohane and Joseph Nye define it as 'network of rules, norms and procedures that regularise behaviour and control its effects'.[20] Other scholars emphasise 'decision-making procedures around which actors' expectations converge'.[21] Paul Diehl combines the various streams and suggests 'an international regime is composed of sets of explicit or implicit principles, norms, rules, and decision-making procedures around which actors' expectations converge in a given area of international relations and which may help to co-ordinate their behaviours'.[22]

Scholars using international regimes have accepted assumptions which, on the one hand rub shoulders with realism and, on the other, depart significantly from functionalism and neo-functionalism. They agree with realists that states are the major actors in world affairs, that states are unitary actors and that anarchy is a major shaping force for state preferences and actions.[23] However, they disagree fundamentally with realists and rejoin forces with functionalists and neo-functionalists over the possibility of international co-operation and the capacities of international institutions. They believe that international institutions can help states to work together. Their departure from functionalism and neo-functionalism lies in their emphasis on the centrality and unitary character of states as actors. Functionalism, associated with the writings of David Mitrany, saw the nation state as a cause of war and proposed to substitute its role with socialised international agencies and their technical experts.[24] Neo-functionalism, put forward by Ernst Haas, viewed interest groups, political parties and the supranational bureaucracy as important actors accelerating the shift of loyalties from the national to the EC level and precipitating a spillover process from economic to political integration.[25] 'From the rationalistic theory perspective, co-operation in one area might spill over into co-operation else-where. However, this will only happen to the extent to which it is conducive to the maximisation of national goals.[26]

On the surface, the concept of international regime does not appear very useful for the study of the EC, because of the wide difference between EC policy-making and any other example of intergovernmental collaboration. Nonetheless, whilst the EC is, in the words of William Wallace, 'less than a federation and more than a regime',[27] and whilst its functions, jurisdictions and resources clearly outpace those of other international organisations, it would be rash to dismiss, as suggested by Susan Strange,[28] the conceptual value of international regimes altogether. The concept of international regime has useful explanations to offer about the conditions under which states co-operate and the reasons why international institutions are established and maintained. It thus has obvious implications for the working of the EC. As Wolfgang Wessels points out, the EC provides for member states higher calculability with fewer risks of getting 'exploited'.[29]

The relevance of the concept of international regimes to the study of EC integration relates particularly to decision-making. The Single European Act (SEA) enables the Council of Ministers to take majority decisions in a number of specified areas. Whether the Council of Ministers will make full use of this and thus speed up EC decision-making, is questioned by the rational approach entailed in the concept of international regimes. The rational approach postulates that 'while any member may block a decision if (effective) unanimity is required, majority voting can give rise to endless unstable coalitions in which, whenever some group appears to have achieved the required majority, one or more of its members is bought off'.[30] We can test the rationalistic approach by considering the extent to which the Council of Ministers resorts to majority decision-making, by what methods (side payments, log rolling, brinkmanship etc), and whether this is done through unanimity rules.

There are, however, limitations to the rationalistic approach which must be recognised. These involve the structural setting of international institutions and the learning of actors. In one of the few examples where rational choice theory has been applied to EC activities (decisions regarding EC technology cooperation) Hugh Ward and Geoffrey Edwards conclude that any explanation which ignored social determinants and past patterns of preference is shallow and that rational choice is insufficient by itself.[31] As Robert Keohane points out 'rationalistic theory accounts better for shifts in the strength of institutions than in the values that they serve to promote.[32] Some attempts have been made, however, by scholars of this school to account for the impact of social processes and for the effect of learning on the preferences of individuals.[33]

The aspect of learning can be observed, for example, in EC monetary co-operation. Britain, France, Ireland and Italy felt disadvantaged by the working of the snake (European currency exchange rate mechanism) whilst Germany was perceived to have gained disportionately from it.[34] The European Monetary System (EMS) was an attempt to rectify the imbalance in gains and losses.[35] Similar efforts, involving transfer payments to states with economic difficulties, were evident in the negotiations of the Intergovernmental Conference on Economic and Monetary Union in 1991.

But in spite of recognising the importance of institutions and 'learning', the differences between the EC and other international organisations make it difficult to draw meaningful inferences from the latter to the former. As Michael Dolan points out, 'because it is sufficiently elastic to include such diverse organisations as OPEC, GATT, the IMF and the EC, and because it emphasises the non-institutional aspects of regimes, a theory of regimes that could do justice to explaining the EC has not appeared'.[36] For William Wallace, the crucial difference between international organisations and the EC is that the latter bears authority and resources which effectively limit the behaviour of the member states and which impose obligations on them which are generally accepted.[37] According to William Wallace, the EC commands resources, distributes benefits, allocates market shares, and adjudicates between conflicting interests.

Moreover, the terms of reference regarding the EC are not clear either. For example, Puchala and Hopkins see the EMS as a specific regime within a wider framework of the Community system, whilst Hoffmann refers to the EC as a formal international regime.[38]

Neo-institutional and federal approaches

An alternative approach which focuses on the structures of the EC whilst incorporating rationalistic explanations, is the neo-institutional one in which a federal analogy is applied. This, as suggested by William Wallace, offers a more appropriate perspective for understanding the nature of the EC political structure (consisting of a relatively developed system of politics and governments) than the loose and limited patterns of international interaction or regimes.[39]

The neo-institutional approach enables one to study the interaction between EC institutions and national governments. It attempts to use a federal analogy in assessing EC developments and the method of decision-making rather than to suggest that the EC is becoming a fully developed federation. In essence it acknowledges that EC achievements do not primarily involve a shift of jurisdictions from national governments to EC institutions but reflect much more an interaction of competences and shared responsibilities between national and EC authorities. The Swiss model of co-operative federalism is seen as relevant because it operates more through focusing the powers of separate states rather than through transferring those powers to a new decision-making centre.[40]

Two different federal systems heve been suggested for EC comparison. William Wallace opts for the US federal system and highlights its regulative and distributive functions. In contrast Fritz Scharpf argues that the West German model is more similar to the EC than the US model. He points out that, unlike US federalism, West German federalism allows the possibility that authority might not be allocated, in zero-sum fashion, to either one (state) or the other level (central) of government, but it might be shared by both.[41]

Scharpf argues that the paradox of European integration – frustration without disintegration and resilience without progress – can be systematically explained as the consequence of a characteristic pattern of policy choices under certain institutional conditions. He suggests that the joint policy-making of both the FRG and the EC suffers from two conditions: (1) central government decisions are directly dependent upon the agreement of constituent governments; and (2) the agreement of constituent governments must be unanimous or nearly unanimous. Scharpf distinguishes between situations of on-going joint decision systems, in which the exit option is foreclosed, and single-shot decisions which allow exit more readily. Under conditions of joint policy-making, the consequences of non-agreement have a considerable impact; such settings may be incapable of reaching effective agreement at the central level, and they may lose the independent capabilities for action of their member governments. Ideally, as Scharpf suggests, a problem-solving approach would be the most suitable and most effective to overcome the 'trap' or sub-optimal outcome of joint decisions. But the preconditions of 'problem-solving', such as orientations towards common goals, values and norms, are difficult to create, and they are easily eroded in cases of conflict, mutual distrust or disagreements over the fairness of distribution rules. Thus reversion to a 'bargaining' style will occur which exacerbates the distribution conflict and reinforces the tendency towards sub-optimal substantive solutions.

Scharpf argues, therefore, that it is the combination of the unanimity rule and a bargaining style which explains the pathologies of public policy associated with joint decisions in the FRG and the EC.

Why a status quo will prevail can be explained, according to Scharpf, by reference to the utility function of member governments for whom present institutional arrangements, in spite of their sub-optimal policy output, seem to represent 'local optima' when compared to either greater centralization or disintegration. To break out of this deadlock or equilibrium, large-scale changes are required in which short-term losses for many or all participants would have to be accepted. This, according to Scharpf, appears unlikely in the EC where the tendencies towards the segregation of interests and ideologies are even more pronounced than in federal systems like the FRG or the USA. There is thus less reason to expect a transfer of the demands, expectations and loyalties of the political elites from national to the Community level. Furthermore, Scharpf argues that on the basis of the German experience one would expect that even the formal relaxation of the unanimity rule in the EC may not make much difference in practice.[42] Scharpf thus surmises that:

as was the case with joint policies in West Germany, the dynamic movement towards greater European integration may have been retarded and, perhaps, reversed, not by the ideological strength of behaviour or by the obstructions of Charles De Gaulle or Mrs Thatcher but by the pathological decision logic inherent in its basic institutional arrangements.[43]

Scharpf concedes that the Community has expanded, and Community law has achieved the effectiveness of the legal order of a federal state, but the price has been 'an ever closer national control exacerbated in the decision process'.[44] The rise of the European Council can be seen as an attempt to assert the control of national policy generalists over the vertical alliances of policy specialists which dominate the Council of Ministers as well as the Commission. Moreover, whilst provisions were made for majority decisions for some SEA items, a number of more important decisions, and all further evolution of the treaty structure, are explicitly reserved for unanimous voting, and the general principle under which all members may exercise a veto in matters affecting their vital national interests remains unchallenged. Ironically, the very limited efforts to strengthen the powers of the European Parliament have not only taken the form of adding another institutional hurdle to EC decision-making, but have reinforced the practical significance of unanimity within the Council of Ministers (where it is necessary to override objections or amendments of the Parliament).[45]

Thus, since the mid-1960s the Council of Ministers has conceded little to the Commission and the EP in terms of decision-making powers and this includes the provisions of the SEA. Although the EP obtained budgetary powers in the 1970s and improved its role in EC decision-making as a consequence of the SEA, it can be seen as marginal. SEA provisions for majority decision-making in the Council of Ministers will (and have) helped the Commission to get more proposals adopted by the Council. But governments have maintained the right of veto, declared that the 1992 deadline for the completion of the internal market is not legally binding,[46] and insisted on playing a role in the implementation of Council of Ministers' decisions (comitology).

Yet there is the question of whether an internal market can be achieved, or the fruits of that market maintained, simply through the mechanism of intergovernmental negotiations, or whether more supranational methods (increased powers of the Commission, the EP and the Court) are needed to achieve the one or to secure the other. Scharpf concurs with William Wallace that the EC is 'stuck' between sovereignty and integration, between management of inter-dependence and acceptance of central decision-making, and between international regime and federation. The view is also held by a number of other scholars that substantive solutions prevail over institutional reforms and that the Community transcends member states, but at the same time remains supported and dependent on them.[47]

However, whilst Scharpf sees little room for a fundamental change (unless there is external interference or a dramatic deterioration in Community performance), William Wallace considers the capacity and priorities of different governments as instrumental for future EC development. But whatever change occurs, according to Wallace, it will be accompanied by the increasing involvement of national bureaucracies and governments in EC decision-making. This implies that COREPER will maintain its gatekeeping function, the number of advisory (regulative) committees will increase, and the role of the Commission and the EP will be kept at a low level. Such a view, however, raises questions about: (1) the state or government as a unitary actor; (2) the link between domestic politics and EC activities; and (3) the role of the Council Presidency. The unitary status of governments is questioned by Everling who sees them as prisoners of domestic and international circumstances.[48]

As admitted by Keohane,[49] rational theory has paid insufficient attention to domestic politics yet a number of scholars have examined the link between international and domestic politics. Among these are James Alt, Peter Gourevitch, Peter Katzenstein, Robert Putnam, and John Zysmann.[50] This empirical research shows, for example, that industrialised states varied in their economic performance during the 1970s in the face of similar challenges (oil shortages, recession and inflation) because of differences in their domestic, political and economic structures. The need to take account of national structures and attitudes in the EC context has been suggested by Helen Wallace and by Simon Bulmer.[51] According to Bulmer, each national polity has a different set of social and economic conditions that shape its national interest and policy content and can vary depending on the subject area. For example, the Danish decision-making procedure tends to be viewed as making negotiators 'at all levels the captives of well defined sectoral interests at the domestic level, thereby creating a system of effective breaks to speedy EC integration.'[52] The unique feature of the Danish Marketing Committee also deserves attention.

Bulmer also suggests that different policy styles prevail and distinguishes between consensus and imposition. This difference depends on the type of political culture, and the strength and effectiveness of governments. Among some of the obvious implications are federal structures as distinguished from unitary structures. For example, the West German federal government must notify states (*Laender*) about educational matters before it can negotiate with its counterparts from other Community countries.

Decision-making and theoretical relevance

National structures and attitudes mingle with EC structures, habits, procedural rules and objectives and represent a network[53] in which a positive sum rather than zero-sum game prevails. According to Wolfgang Wessels:

This EC pattern of administrative and political interactions reflects a trend by which member states 'pool' their sovereignties and mix them with competences of the EC into a system to which the notion of 'co-operative federalism' can be applied. Competences are not shifted from the national to EC level without any compensation ... but a different pattern can be observed. The more intensive are the forms and stronger are the impacts of the common policy making, the more extensive and intensive are the organisational devices for access and the influence which national officials and politicians preserve for themselves.[54]

More theoretical work is therefore necessary on joint EC decision-making.[55] This should include an understanding of how bargains are struck in EC decision-making and an assessment of the accumulated patterns of behaviour of the main protagonists in the process.[56]

As part of such an undertaking, the role of the EC Council Presidency in EC decision-making will be explored in the following chapters. The Council Presidency is at the nexus between national and Community politics. The Council Presidency helps to facilitate administrative and political interaction between the two layers and has influence on the pace and direction of EC development.

The role of the Council Presidency reflects the importance of national actors and inter-state bargains in EC decision-making but it also highlights the existence of an intense and effective relationship with the Commission and the EP. The Council Presidency is thus an interesting object of study for intergovernmentalists, neo-functionalists and those interested in EC decision-making. The dual interest (national and Community) held by the Presidency as well as its sharing of functions with the Commission are the crucial aspects to be considered here. They take us to the core of the debate between intergovernmentalism and neo-functionalism on how integration will proceed. For intergovernmentalists, as for realists, converging national interests, inter-state bargains and constraints on further EC reform represent the main guidelines for the pace and direction of EC integration as well as the autonomy and influence of national leaders vis-à-vis the EC.[57] Neo-functionalists, in contrast, emphasise the importance of supranational actors and transnational interest groups in the process of integration. They also stress the importance of task expansion into new sectors in order to protect gains already achieved. In short, whereas neo-functionalists emphasise the up-grading of the common interest, the linking of issues and the role of package deals, intergovernmentalists highlight the lowest common denominator and the role of bargaining[58] in EC decision-making.

What role, then, have national governments, as distinct from the Commission and transnational interest groups, played in the negotiations and content of the SEA? Equally, has the Council Presidency exercised an expansive or a restrictive role in the implementation of the SEA?

The SEA is a remarkable event in EC development and is an important test of theoretical models. Whilst not bringing about a European federation, the SEA reinstates quasi-constitutional provisions, out of favour in the EC since the infamous Luxembourg compromise of 1966. Besides naming the policy sectors in which the EC will either renew or newly introduce its co-operative efforts, the SEA deals with constitutional competences and majority decision-making. Nonetheless, one should keep in perspective both the limitations of the SEA, and one should not underestimate the difficulties which will arise over the actual implementation of the provisions agreed in 1986. On the other hand, far-reaching SEA implementation, (particularly if it were accompanied by an increase in the powers of the Commission, the EP and the Court of Justice), would indicate that realist assumptions, about the centrality of the state as the main actor in EC matters, may have become less relevant. It might also demonstrate that the EC will be able to overcome the 'trap' and pathology described by Fritz Scharpf.

The evidence on the content of and bargaining over the SEA (and the role of the Council Presidency in the implementation of the SEA) will be used to shed more light on the theoretical relevance of either intergovernmentalism (realism) or neo-functionalism for the study of integration. The main focus in the following chapters, however, will be on the process of EC decision-making and on the neo-institutional approach outlined above. In other words, the analysis will centre on how EC decision-making proceeds, how tasks are shared between national and EC authorities, and what role the Presidency plays in such a co-operative federalist framework.

Conclusion

Though the EC has expanded in size and responsibilities since its inception in the 1950s, no single theoretical framework can yet explain why progress has been achieved in certain periods and not in others, or why co-operation has occurred in some policy areas and not in others. On the contrary, at least two contesting approaches prevail under the banners of neo-functionalism and inter-governmentalism. The former sees the progression of the EC as confirmation of the cumulative logic of sector spillover and an increasing transfer of competences from the national to the EC level. Inter-governmentalism, on the other hand, stresses that the pace and direction of EC co-operation is in accordance with national interests and is achieved through arrangements such as the Council of Ministers and the European Council over which member states have full control. Neither approach seems to capture adequately the existing overlap in decision-making between national and Community authorities, the sharing of joint tasks and interests, and the fusion of competences between the national and Community level.

Models derived from decision-making in federal systems, particularly in the form of co-operative federalism, offer interesting comparative perspectives on EC decision-making. Also known as neo-institutionalism, such an approach will help to assess the important role the Council Presidency plays in EC development. An analysis of the forces and actors involved in the negotiation, content and implementation of the SEA will help to shed more light on both the theoretical debate about integration and the impact of the Council Presidency in EC decision-making. This will be the task in the following chapters.

Notes

1   Among the leading contributors to this approach were: K.C. Wheare, *Federal Governments*, 4th edition, London, 1963; David Mitrany, *A Working Peace System*, Chicago, 1966; Ernst B. Haas, *The Uniting of Europe, Political, Economic and Social Forces, 1950–1957*, Stanford, 1958; and Leon Lindberg, *The Political Dynamics of European Economic Integration*, Stanford, 1963.

2   Among the major works commenting on the problems of theorising about the politics of the European Community, see Leon Lindberg and Stuart Scheingold, eds, *Regional Integration, Theory and Research*, Harvard, 1971; Charles Pentland, *International Theory and European Integration*, London, 1973; Reginald Harrison, *Europe in Question*, London, 1974; Paul Taylor, *The Limits of European Integration*, London, 1983.

3   Robert O. Keohane and Joseph S. Nye, Jr, *Power and Interdependence: World Politics in Transition*, Boston, 1977.

4   Oran R. Young, 'International regimes: problems of concept formation', *World Politics*, XXXII, 1980; Stephen D. Krasner, ed., *International Regimes*, Ithaca, 1983.

5   For major works on realism see, for example, E.H. Carr, *The Twenty Years Crisis, 1919–1939: An Introduction to the Study of International Relations*, London and New York, 1964; Hans J. Morgenthau, *Politics Among Nations: The Struggle for Power and Peace*, 5th edition, New York, 1973; Kenneth N. Waltz, *Man, the State and War: A Theoretical Analysis*, New York, 1959.

6   See Carole Webb, 'Introduction: variations on a theoretical theme', in Helen Wallace, William Wallace and Carole Webb, eds, *Policy Making in the European Communities*, Chichester, 1977; and Taylor, *The Limits of European Integration*, especially chapter 3.

7   Alan S. Milward, *The Reconstruction of Western Europe 1945–1951*, London, 1987.

8   Ernst B. Haas, 'The obsolescence of regional integration theory', Research Series, 25, Institute of International Studies, University of California, Berkeley, 1975.

9   For an excellent analysis on increasing state functions, see Peter Flora, ed., *Growth to Limits: The Western European Welfare State since World War II*, IV, Berlin, 1987.

10   Stanley Hoffmann, 'Obstinate or obsolete? The fate of the nation-state and the case of Western Europe', *Daedalus*, 1966, pp. 862–915.

11   William Wallace, 'Less than a federation, more than a regime: the Community as a political system', in H. Wallace et al., eds, *Policy Making in the European Community*, 2nd edition, Chichester, 1983, pp. 403–36; and Fritz Scharpf, 'The joint-decision trap: lessons from German federalism and European integration', *Public Administration*, LXVI, 1988, pp. 239–78.

12   Wolfgang Wessels, 'The growth of the EC system – a product of the dynamics of modern European states? A plea for a more comprehensive approach', paper presented at the International Political Science Association, Washington, 28 August to 1 September 1988.

13   Haas, 'The obsolescence of regional integration theory'.

14   For a review of this perspective see Joseph Grieco, 'Anarchy and the limits of cooperation', *International Organization*, XLII, 3, 1988, pp. 485–507.

15   See Fulvio Attina, 'Institutions and identity: rethinking European integration with a neo-institutional approach', paper delivered at the ISA Convention in London, April 1989.

16   See Stanley Hoffmann, 'Reflections on the national state in Western Europe today', *Journal of Common Market Studies*, XXI, 1982, pp. 21–37; and R. Jordan and W. Feld, *Europe in the Balance*, 1986.

17   Donald Puchala, cited by C. Webb, 'Theoretical perspectives', in H. Wallace, et al., eds, *Policy Making in the European Community*, 1983.

18   See, for example, Oran Young, 'International regimes'; and Krasner, ed., *International Regimes*, 1983.

19   See, for example, Donald J. Puchala and Raymond F. Hopkins, 'International regimes: lessons from inductive analysis', in Krasner, ed., *International Regimes*, pp. 61–91.

20   Keohane and Nye, *Power and Interdependence*.

21   Friedrich   Kratochwil   and   John   G.   Ruggie,   'International

organization: the state of the art', in Paul F. Diehl ed., *The Politics of International Organizations: Patterns and Insights*, Chicago, 1989, pp. 17–27.

22   Diehl, ed., *The Politics of International Organizations*, p. 15. See also Krasner, ed., *International Regimes*.

23   For example, Axelrod and Keohane point out that there is no common government to enforce rules, and by the standards of domestic study, international institutions are weak. Robert Axelrod and Robert O. Keohane, 'Achieving cooperation under anarchy: strategies and institutions', *World Politics*, XXXVIII, 1985, p. 226.

24   Mitrany, *A Working Peace System*.

25   Haas, *The Uniting of Europe*.

26   Hugh Ward, 'The relevance of rational choice in decision-making', working paper, University of Essex, 1989.

27   W. Wallace, 'Less than a federation more than a regime'.

28   Susan Strange, 'Cave hic dragones: a critique of regime analysis', in Diehl, ed., The Politics of International Organizations, pp. 51–65.

29   W. Wessels, 'The growth of the EC system'.

30   Ward, 'The relevance of rational choice'.

31   Hugh Ward and Geoffrey Edwards, 'Chicken and technology: the politics of the EC's budget for research and development', *Review of International Studies*, XVI, 1990, pp. 111–31.

32   Robert O. Keohane, 'International institutions: two approaches', *International Studies Quarterly*, XXXII, 1988, p. 391.

33   Keohane, 'International institutions'; see also Friedrich Kratochwil and John G. Ruggie, 'International organization: the state of the art', in Diehl, ed., *The Politics of International Organizations*, pp. 17–27.

34   See Loukas Tsoukalis, *The Politics and Economics of European Monetary Integration*, London, 1977.

35   See Peter Ludlow, *The Making of the European Monetary System*, London, 1982; Peter Coffey, *The European Monetary System: Past, Present, and Future*, Dordrecht, 1984.

36   See Michael Dolan, 'Dialectical political economy and European integration: critique of extant theory and a research design', paper presented at the ISA Convention in London, April 1989; see also Martin Rochester, 'The rise and fall of International Organization as a field of study', *International Organization*, 1987, p. 803.

37   William Wallace, 'Europe as a Confederation: the Community and the Nation State', *Journal of Common Market Studies*, XXI, 1982, pp. 57–68.

38   Puchala and Hopkins, 'International Regimes'; and Hoffmann, 'Obstinate or obsolete?'.

39   W. Wallace, 'Europe as a Confederation'.

40   Wessels, 'The growth of the EC system'.

41   Scharpf, 'The joint-decision trap', p. 242.

42   Ibid., p. 269.

43   Ibid.

44   Ibid.

45 Scharpf, 'The joint-decision trap', pp. 268–9.

46 For further details see note 25 in Chapter 1.

47 See, for example, Ulrich Everling, 'Possibilities and limits of European integration', *Journal of Common Market Studies*, 1980, pp. 217–28; Joseph Weiler, 'Community, member states and European integration'; and Wessels, 'The growth of the EC system'.

48 Everling, 'Possibilities and limits'.

49 Keohane, 'International institutions: two approaches'.

50 James Alt, 'Crude politics: oil and the political economy of unemployment in Britain and Norway, 1970–1985', *British Journal of Political Science*, 1987; Peter Gourevitch, 'The second image reversed: the international source of domestic politics', *International Organization*, XXXII, 1978, pp. 881–911; Peter Katzenstein, *Between Power and Plenty: Foreign Economic Policies of Advanced Industrial States*, Madison, 1978; and Peter Katzenstein, *Small States in World Markets: Industrial Policy in Europe*, Ithaca, 1985; Robert Putnam, 'Diplomacy and domestic politics: the logic of two-level games', *International Organization*, XLII, 1988, pp. 427–60; and John Zysmann, *Governments, Markets and Growth – Financial Systems and the Politics of Industrial Change*, Ithaca, 1983.

51 Helen Wallace, 'The impact of the European Community on national policy making, in H. Wallace et al., eds., *Policy Making in the European Community; and Simon Bulmer, The Domestic Structure of European Community Policy-Making in West Germany*, New York, 1986.

52 Roger B. Selbert, *Compatible Two Sphere Integration: The Simultaneous Danish Participation in the European Communities and Nordic Cooperation*, published in 1979 with the Commission of the European Communities.

53 For a description of the EC as a network form of organisation, see particularly the contributions by Albert Bressand and Kalypso Nicolaidis 'Regional integration in a networked world economy', and Robert O. Keohane and Stanley Hoffmann, 'Conclusions: Community politics and institutional change', in William Wallace, ed., *The Dynamics of European Integration*, London, 1990, pp. 27–49 and 276–300 respectively.

54 Wolfgang Wessels, 'Administrative interaction', in W. Wallace, ed., *The Dynamics of European Integration*, p. 238.

55 This is also suggested by Keohane and Hoffmann, 'Conclusions: Community politics', p. 284.

56 Helen Wallace, 'Making multilateral negotiations work', in W. Wallace, ed., *The Dynamics of European Integration*, p. 214.

57 Andrew Moravcsik, 'Negotiating the Single European Act: interests and conventional statecraft in the European Community', *International Organization*, XLV, 1, 1991, p. 27.

58 This is particularly well demonstrated in Wayne Sandholtz and John Zysmann, 'Recasting the EC bargain', *World Politics*, XLII, 1989, pp. 95–128.

3

Motives, importance and implications of the SEA

Introduction

Expansion and reform of the Treaties of Rome has been on the agenda since the late 1960s. Various signals were given to this effect in EC summit meetings, (especially in 1969, 1972 and 1974), and a number of reports were drawn up such as the Vedel Report,[1] the Tindemans' Report,[2] and the Three Wise Men Report[3] in the 1970s. However only a few actual attempts were made during that period to expand and reform the Treaties. These involved the Werner Plan or 'snake' monetary arrangement (1971), the budgetary powers of the European Parliament (1970,1975), and the EMS (1979). Given the severity of the economic problems in the 1970s and the prevailing differences in economic structures, performance and policy aims, (itself an indication of the lack of EC progress in economic integration), the absence of far-reaching reforms was perhaps not so surprising. Governments, faced with mounting pressures to stimulate economic growth, maintain welfare demands, and protect the social and political cohesion of society, sought individual remedies or engaged in a beggar-thy-neighbour approach, rather than seeking collective agreements. In this situation, governments found it expedient to characterise the EC as either too costly, too wasteful, too bureaucratic/technocratic, too biased, too rigid or a combination of these complaints. In short, the EC was portrayed as being, at best a nuisance and, at worst, detrimental to the national economic interest.

How then did the EC move from this situation of the 1970s to a collective, constructive, and dynamic response in the mid-1980s? Did the leading national actors experience or learn that national solutions were too limited in the face of economic interdependence and the globalisation of economies? Did they recognise that on a regional comparison, the USA and Japan seemed to be performing much better economically than the 'Eurosclerosis'-marked EC; or that they needed 'economies of scale', diminished administration costs in trade interaction, and co-ordinated research and development programmes? The realisation by governments that individual policies were insufficient and needed to be supplemented or replaced, therefore, appears important. But whilst actor learning seems to be a central variable in explaining the increased co-operation among member states, it does not sufficiently explain: (1) the diversity of forces which brought about the SEA; (2) the negotiations and trade-offs comprising the formation of the SEA; and (3) the advantages and disadvantages associated with the SEA as an instrument for further integration. It is the task of this chapter to explore these three aspects.

Economic malaise and forces for reform

The process of EC economic integration had developed largely upon the economic prosperity of the 1960s. The severe economic difficulties of the 1970s were, therefore, a crucial test of the EC's existence and its future. Having experienced severe economic problems for ten years and having failed during that period to make any notable progress in EC decision-making and policy-making, why did 1984 become the year when economic divergence was checked and integration reintroduced? The reason for this change can be found in emerging and changing government attitudes in which the 'learning' factor played a crucial role. Three sets of interrelated factors appear to have influenced government attitudes: (1) economic problems and policies; (2) EC institutional and enlargement questions; and (3) political issues. As will be shown below, different countries attributed different weights to each factor. However, rather than establishing the saliency of each factor, this chapter is concerned with their cumulative effect and bargaining implications in the adoption of the SEA. In what follows, each factor will be briefly examined.

National economic problems and policies
The economic malaise of the 1970s and the associated economic divergence of the EC has received extensive treatment in the literature[4] and will only be dealt with briefly here. Faced initially with oil

shortages and rising oil prices, EC countries, like most industrialised countries, experienced what is generally described as 'stagflation' (high unemployment and high inflation). Low economic growth rates were associated with lower investment which in turn affected a variety of sectors such as welfare, research and development programmes, and regional development. The pressure on governments was, therefore, heightened as providers of services and at the same time acted to re-inforce a downward economic spiral. Moreover, the EC governments, unlike those of the USA or Japan, had greater welfare responsibilities and demands to meet.[5] Unlike these two countries they also had, generally, a more demanding and politically motivated trade union force to contend with, for example, in terms of wage demands,[6] reduced working hours, worker participation or the introduction of new technologies. Anti-inflationary, monetarist or austerity policies were, therefore, more difficult to administer, and contributed largely to a relatively high turnover of government in the 1970s and early 1980s.[7]

Though EC countries paralleled American and Japanese efforts in reducing inflation, they could not match them on job creation,[8] economic growth, investment patterns and technological innovation. Indeed there were indications that the EC market was successfully penetrated by American and Japanese high-technology industries without having any corresponding export success in those countries.[9] EC countries found it difficult to adjust to fluctuating, mostly falling, dollar rates and fluctuating interest rates.

The prevailing economic stagnation[10] was accompanied by a loss of international competitiveness. Raw material dependency, unit costs, industrial relations, and technological innovation were factors which seemed to give competitors like the USA, Japan or newly industrialised countries the edge over EC countries in a number of sectors such as textiles and electronics. In addition, EC countries were burdening themselves, for half of their external trade (intra-Community trade), entailed heavy administrative costs in frontier formalities, and hidden obstacles to trade. For example, European companies needed to spend about $400 million every year on transport formalities at frontiers – in some cases up to seventy different forms had to be completed for a consignment of goods to reach a destination within the EC.[11] In addition, different national standards and regulations added up to 12 per cent to the final price.[12] Government protectionism was, and is, also a factor inhibiting free trade. For example, it was estimated that 400,000 jobs could be created by the liberalisation of public procurement alone.[13] With the cost of the EC's fragmented market exceeding 200 billion ECUs, the Cecchini report correctly noted that the 'common market became a term used with growing embarrassment and decreasing accuracy to describe the trading and market relationship between EC member countries'.[14] Not surprisingly, therefore, the absence of a single market and its implications for economies of scale in research and development, manufacturing and commercial terms was identified as a main factor in the loss of international competitiveness. Indeed in the early 1980s leading West European industrialists, in a series of round table discussions, began to argue that with slackening economies, wasteful and costly features of a 'non-common market' should be replaced with a single market in which goods, services, capital and people could move freely.[15] Parallel recommendations were advanced by the EP with its Draft Treaty for a European Union.[16] Overall the EP reform plans, however, went well beyond the single market, by providing a constitutional blueprint for a European Union. A more modest, though persistent, campaign was undertaken by the Commission who reminded member states of the dangers of economic divergence and the need to introduce co-ordinated measures.

Furthermore, greater co-ordination of external trade issues, whether through the Multifibre Agreement (MFA)[17] or the Lomé Convention, had produced some positive results. Such co-ordination had also proved useful in coping with the steel crisis.[18] Importantly, however, the economic (Keynesian) policies tried by France and Greece in the early 1980s, like those by the British Labour government in the 1970s, were seen as too isolated.[19] This helped to establish a convergence on monetarist policies and the collective pursuit of such policies among governments. To some EC countries, the EMS appeared helpful in checking the fluctuating rates of the US dollar and in complementing monetarist (anti-inflationary) policies, and thus they felt that a strengthening of this mechanism and the use of the ECU was desirable.[20] The success of neo-liberal economic policies such as those pursued in Britain under Mrs Thatcher, for example, was also significant because they needed Community backing whilst at the same time the policies stood as a model for EC-wide consideration.

Whilst a consensus was emerging about the need to overcome

individual national economic policy moves and to replace them with a co-ordinated approach, member states were facing another acute problem in the shape of a protracted EC decision-making machinery which produced 'sub-optimal' results.[21]

EC institutional and enlargement questions

As a consequence of the 1966 Luxembourg compromise and the economic divergence of the 1970s, national governments had reasserted their role in EC decision-making. Moreover, EC decision-making had become very complex, cumbersome and slow. Most decisions, even those involving minor issues, were taken on the basis of the lowest common denominator. With the Commission being largely sidelined or enmeshed in governmental negotiation and bargaining, a number of largely intergovernmental structures emerged or assumed greater importance. Amongst these were Advisory Committees, COREPER, Technical Councils, European Councils, and the Presidency, which challenged the authority and independence of the Commission. These new structures, and the increasing involvement of national bureaucracies in EC decision-making, contributed to a 'pooling of sovereignties' in which national interest, rather than being transferred to the supranational domain, was safeguarded by the member states. The insistence on unanimity and the existence of an unwieldy network of channels and actors resulted in prolonged bargaining and inefficient policy-making. Unsuccessful attempts both to reform the CAP and the EC budget, especially on its revenue side, reflected this dilemma. Whilst this situation was in itself highly unsatisfactory, the prospect of the EC enlarging to include Portugal and Spain appeared to worsen this still further. The antidote to the notion of 'wider but weaker' was provided by the EP's draft Treaty for a European Union which, among other things, wanted to restrict the use of the 'veto' and introduce majority decision-making as widely as possible. Some of the EP's proposals, for example, those on enhancing its own powers, found support in countries such as Italy and West Germany, but overall the EP draft Treaty raised fears of rapid supranationalism. Nonetheless, some member states felt that a reaction to the EP plan was in order and in line with the need for EC institutional and decision-making reforms.

Political issues

Economic and institutional factors, however, were not the only determinants of EC reforms. Environmentalists, campaigning amongst other things against the expansion of nuclear power stations, and anti-nuclear weapons protestors also influenced the thinking and action of government. Various studies have shown that Western Europeans have, like citizens of other Western countries, undergone substantial value changes.[22] Economic prosperity and increased levels of education, especially in the 1960s, are seen as the main agents of these changes which have affected pre-adult socialisation. Subsequently, there is, for example, greater concern over the environment and with detente. This concern helped to launch a number of 'Green' parties, of which the West German Greens became particularly important. However, the rise of the latter and the occurrence of a strong peace movement sparked-off fears, primarily in neighbouring France, of West Germany turning neutral and of weakening its ties with the EC and NATO.[23] In response to these anxieties there was a heightening of Franco–German co-operation, (including security issues), a revival of the WEU, and the declaration of the EC Stuttgart summit of 1983 to strengthen European Political Co-operation (EPC) and to extend it to security considerations.[24] However, there was also concern that the planned American SDI programme could exclude Western Europe or not give it a 'fair' share of the technological know-how associated with its establishment. French calls for a European response to the SDI, in the shape of Eureka and the ESA, therefore found the support of other EC member states by 1984. There was also a concern that the EC was not responding to international events coherently and efficiently. Undoubtedly, this was prompted by events surrounding the deployment of medium-range nuclear missiles in Europe, the American request for greater 'burden-sharing' in the defence of Western Europe, and conflicts in the Middle East, Central America, and South Africa.

Negotiations

Agreeing on the need for reforms was only half of the battle. With each country wanting something to which another seemed to be diametrically opposed, the successful outcome to any agreement could only be in the form of a package deal or compromise. Most differences occurred over the extent to which: (1) new Community-wide policies should be introduced;[25] (2) powers should be given to institutions such as the Commission, the EP, and the Court of Justice in the phasing-in and working of these new policies; and (3) majority decision-making should be used in adopting these new policies and, by implication, the extent to which the 'veto' should be maintained. With regard to policies, differences occurred, for example, over the intended scope of the internal market provisions, the possibility of derogations, and the deadline of 1992 and its 'binding' status. Other differences involved the inclusion of monetary, environmental and social policies. For example, Britain, West Germany and the Nether-lands expressed opposition to far-reaching measures with regard to monetary policy. Denmark, on the other hand, wanted to go further than other countries with regard to social policy harmonisation, e.g. minimal measures for safety at work. Denmark also wanted to give member states an opportunity to opt for more advanced measures if they so wished. Agreement was more easily forthcoming on the need to transfer resources to the economically deprived regions, or those which would suffer from the working of the internal market, though the actual amount and method of payment led to difficulties.[26] Interests converged also on the need for R&D programmes, though, once again, details could not be worked out. A major stumbling block occurred over the inclusion of EPC. The negotiations in the Intergovernmental Conference of 1985 were based on a proposal by Britain and a Franco–German proposal which had been tabled at the Milan summit of June 1985 while two more proposals were pre-sented by Italy and the Netherlands. All proposals agreed on the codification of common practices within the sphere of EPC. How-ever, right from the beginning it became apparent that there were differences as to the proposed objectives and structure of EPC. The Franco–German proposals and, in particular, the Italian proposals were strongly worded in favour of increased co-ordination on all aspects of security. In contrast, the British proposal ('Howe Plan') stressed 'co-operation', 'regular consultations' and 'exchange of information'[27] – expressing worries, for example, that co-operation on technological aspects of security could interfere with the American SDI programme. There were also differences over the size and authority of an EPC secretariat. Finally, there was disagreement over the extent to which links between EPC and NATO and the WEU should be maintained. These proposals were heavily criticised by Ireland (because of neutrality) and by Denmark and Greece.

With regard to decision-making, Greece and Denmark were generally opposed to majority voting, in whatever form, while West Germany, Ireland, the Netherlands, and the United Kingdom opposed majority voting in specific areas such as taxation and minimum standards of health and safety. Greece and Denmark together with Britain found proposals for greater EP powers unacceptable. In contrast, Italy pressed most strongly for EP co-legislative powers.[28]

The SEA, then, is a political compromise between policy and institutional objectives, the desire to increase Community competences and decision-making efficiency and the need to maintain national control.[29] The outcome was a package deal comprising elements of both. The package reflected both domestic considerations and the give and take bargaining of member states. Following Putnam, we can detect an interrelationship between domestic factors and Community-level bargaining, in which the creation of 'win sets' becomes, on the one hand, a function of domestic coalitions and institutions and on the other negotiating strategies and skills at the Community level. Accordingly, at national level 'domestic groups seek to maximise their interests by pressuring the government to adopt favourable policies, and politicians seek power by constructing coalitions among these groups'. At Community level 'national governments seek to maximise their own freedom to satisfy domestic pressures while minimising the adverse consequences of foreign developments'.[30] Games at both levels (national and Community) are played simultaneously. Equally, as seen by Putnam, the emphasis in such 'win sets' is on the negotiating process, in which leaders, because they have to communicate at both levels, play a crucial role.[31]

The SEA negotiating process was based on broad coalitions at national level between governments and the business community. These centred on the need to promote liberal market forces (via Community means) and to ensure that monetarist policy objectives were upheld throughout the Community in order to revive member states economies and competitiveness. The considerable economic interdependence among member states, and the realisation (learning) that all played according to the same rules, both on internal market matters and foreign policy issues, became a significant determinant of the negotiations.

What does the SEA entail?

The SEA is the first major successful attempt to amend and expand the EC treaty provisions.[32] Though never short of grandiose schemes, like the announcement at the 1972 Paris summit meeting to establish a European Union by 1980, the actual steps taken by the EC between 1969 and 1984 were either small with regard to treaty revisions or involved policy arrangements of an intergovernmental type. Among the former are the 1975 revision of the budgetary powers of the European Parliament. Intergovernmental arrangements were made, for example, with regard to the monetary field (snake and EMS) and EPC. The SEA, on the other hand, introduces far-reaching changes to the institutions of the EC as well as the Community as a whole. The foundations to this undertaking were laid at: (1) the 1984 Fontainebleau European Council, which initiated an institutional committee (consisting of national governmental representatives) whose objective was to explore the prospects for treaty reforms;[33] (2) the 1985 Milan European Council, which, following the recommendations of the institutional (Dooge) committee, decided on the holding of an Intergovernmental Conference;[34] and (3) the European Council at Luxembourg, which finalised the text for the adoption of the SEA and recommended it for signature to the member governments in February 1986. The EP draft Treaty on European Union, the 1985 Commission's White Paper on the formation of an internal market,[35] and a few national governmental memoranda provided valuable input to both the work of the institutional committee and the 1985 Intergovernmental Conference.

The document, 'Single European Act and Final Act', falls into two parts. The first part deals with the Single Act proper and has four titles and thirty-four articles. These titles relate to: common provisions; provisions amending the Treaties establishing the European Communities; provisions on European Political Co-operation in the sphere of foreign policy; and general and final provisions. The second part of the document, the Final Act, lists some twenty joint or unilateral declarations by governments, which express reservations, derogations and interpretations on Articles contained in the Single European Act proper where there were differences of opinion by one or more member statess. In the following the amendments and 'new' provisions will be briefly examined.

Institutional matters cannot clearly be separated from policy matters. For example, policy areas coming under the legal framework of the EC enhance the Commission's role in initiating policy, or enable the Court of Justice to deliver judgments in cases of dispute. However, for analytical reasons we will treat institutional matter as distinct from the policy field. A start will be made on the latter.

Policy provisions

Title two of the SEA outlines six policy areas: completion of the internal market; monetary capacity; social policy; economic and social cohesion; research and technological development; and environment. Title three deals with EPC. Let us look briefly at each of these fields.

Internal market
The SEA breaks new ground by giving a definition of 'internal market': 'The internal market shall compose an area without internal frontiers in which the free movement of goods, persons, services and capital is ensured in accordance with the provisions of the Treaty' (Article 13). As laid down in the 1985 Commission's White Paper, it seeks to eliminate physical, technical and fiscal barriers. Under physical barriers fall customs and border controls for persons and goods. Technical barriers involve, for example, obstacles created by different standards, and professional qualification requirements. Fiscal barriers relate to turnover taxes, excise duties and other forms of indirect taxation. To ensure a speedy introduction of these measures, majority voting is specified for a number of provisions. The target date of 31 December 1992 is, however, not legally binding. One of the declarations of the Final Act states that 'setting the date of 31 December 1992 does not create an automatic legal effect'. This provision eliminates the possibility that in 1993 governments can be taken to the Court of Justice in the event that national legislation has not been adjusted in time.[36]

Monetary capacity
Formerly, there were neither specific monetary obligations contained in the treaties, nor were the general references mentioned therein adequate to cope with the economic problems of the 1970s.

The EMS had developed outside the EC framework. The SEA stipulates that member states will take the necessary actions in order to ensure the convergence of their economies. The EMS and the ECU are mentioned by name but further institutional changes in this area require Article 236 of the Treaty for alteration, e. g. an amendment procedure based on unanimity.

Social policy

The SEA urges member states to pay particular attention to encouraging social policy improvements, especially in the working environment. The new Article 118A not only calls for closer co-ordination of action as regards health and safety of workers but it also enables the Council of Ministers to set 'minimum requirements for gradual implementation'. This solves a long-standing problem between the Council of Ministers and the Commission with regard to the establishment of the institution responsible for drawing the guidelines of social policy.[37] Allowance is also made for upgraded protection standards (by individual member states) as long as they do not contradict the treaty, i.e. constitute a form of trade barrier. Finally, the SEA social policy provisions refer to a dialogue at European level between management and labour, with a view to 'relations based on agreement'.

Economic and social cohesion

In five new articles to the treaty, the SEA calls for a reduction of regional disparities by means of economic policy co-ordination and rationalisation of the Structural Funds and the European Investment Bank. It also defines and institutionalises the Regional Development Fund, and calls for 'significant increases in the allocation to the Structural Funds'. In short, it aims at producing economic cohesion by reducing the gap between rich and poor and giving economic support to the economically disadvantaged or periphery states.

Research and technological development

The basic aim of the eleven articles introduced with regard to research and technological development is to increase the competitiveness of European industry in the international market in parallel with the opening of the internal market. It also seeks further Community co-operation, and policy co-ordination, in the field by removing obstacles to cross-country research (Article 130 F). Strictly

speaking, the EC had already begun to respond to the R&D challenge with the establishment of the ESPRIT, RACE, BRITE, and
EUREKA programmes.[38] However, some of these programmes were
either outside EC or Commission competency. Among the SEA
provisions are calls for links between academic, research establishment and the business community. Multi-annual R&D
framework programmes are envisaged which will be broken down
into a series of specific programmes. The financing of each programme will be established at the time of its adoption. The Commission is to liaise with member states in their national research programmes and is entrusted to take initiatives in order to further their
co-ordination (Article 130 H).

Environment

Three new articles are added to the treaties with regard to environmental issues, entailing the 'principles of preventive action', and the
'polluter pays' both of which make environmental protection a
component of all other Community policies. Before specific actions
are taken, the Commission is requested to acquire scientific and
technical data. It is also to assess differing regional conditions,
potential costs, and the economic development of the Commmunity
as a whole. The principle of 'subsidiarity'[39] is safeguarded in that
action at Community level will be taken if the tasks to be carried out
can be completed more successfully at an EC rather than national
level (Article 130 R). Also, member states are allowed to introduce
more stringent measures, as long as they do not represent technical
barriers or interfere with the principle of free competition.

New provisions

The SEA has both legitimised the previous practice of EPC and
established some new provisions. In accordance with previous tradi-
tions, member governments 'endeavour' to form a common policy,
by means of consultations on any matter of foreign policy. What is
new is that 'the external policies of the EC and the policies agreed
under EPC must be consistent': putting the onus jointly on the
Commission and the Council Presidency to ensure coherence
between the two systems. In fact, the SEA permits the General Affairs
Council, composed of the foreign ministers, to discuss EPC matters,
thus further enhancing the unity of the two systems.[40] In addition,
the SEA breaks new ground with its reference to the need for co-

ordination and co-operation 'on the political, technological and economic aspects of security'. Finally, provision has been made for extraordinary meetings which may be called with forty-eight hours notice at the request of at least three member states. The Commission is to be fully associated with the proceedings of the EPC but because EPC has its own structure, the Commission's role is restricted. EPC initiatives and conduct is mainly the task of the Council Presidency, aided by the newly established EPC secretariat, the Political Committee (which prepares Ministers' meetings) and the Correspondents' Group (charged with organisational aspects of EPC). The quasi-institutionalisation of EPC represents a concession to national sovereignty. But, though it is an exhibition of solidarity or a statement of intent to the outside, its impact is restricted by the unanimity rule which harbours and protects diverging national foreign policy interests. Under these circumstances, it may be no more than an attempt to minimise foreign policy divergence or disunity within the EC.

Institutional provisions

The need for institutional reform has been one of the long standing issues in the EC. As D. Edward noted:

The institutional debate was an obstacle to the achievement of concrete results because it was in many ways a destructive element in relations between the Community and the member states and between the institutions of the Community themselves. It was, in a word, an alibi for inaction.[41]

The institutional debate had centered around five themes: (1) the role of the EP, both with respect to its relationship with the Council of Ministers and the Commission, and its consultative and legislative capacity; (2) the Commission's powers of management and implementation in Community policy; (3) voting arrangements in the Council of Ministers; (4) the institutionalisation of the European Council; and (5) the workload of the Court of Justice. How were these issues settled? The last two proved to be the least contentious and will be looked at first.

Article 2 of the SEA institutionalises European Councils which, since 1975, have become regular meetings of the head of states and governments of the member states. These bi-annual meetings are being chaired by the representative of the country which has the Presidency of the Council of Ministers. Article 140 A enables the

Council of Ministers to attach to the Court, on the Court's request, a court with jurisdiction to hear cases brought by natural or legal persons. This court is composed of judges appointed by the governments and its rules of procedure are drawn by the Court of Justice and require the unanimous approval of the Council of Ministers.

With regard to the European Parliament, the SEA made a number of amendments. The term 'Assembly' is replaced by 'Parliament' and the phrase 'after consulting with the Assembly' is replaced by 'in co-operation with the European Parliament'. Article 6, amending Article 149 of the Treaty, proposes a new triangular co-operation procedure between the Council, Commission and the EP for ten specific articles,[42] which gives the EP the opportunity of two readings. Under the co-operation procedure the Council of Ministers, without being subject to a time constraint, adopts its 'common' position on a Commission proposal and on the EP submission (first reading). At first reading, the EP is not bound by any time constraints. The 'common' position, which can be adopted by majority voting, is then sent to the EP, which has three months to either accept (by simple majority) or reject/amend it by an absolute majority of its members. Failure by the EP to comply with this is considered as a tacit acceptance. A rejected EP decision can only be overruled by a unanimous Council of Ministers vote, otherwise the proposal will fall. The amendments of the EP second reading will go to the Commission, which has one month to re-draft and re-submit it to the Council of Ministers. The latter then has three months to adopt it by a qualified majority vote, or change it unanimously.[43] Failure to comply with this time limit implies automatic rejection by the Council of Ministers of the proposals. Should the Commission choose to incorporate EP amendments, the Council can, through a unanimous decision, alter them. On the other hand, should the Commission ignore the EP amendments, the Council can instate them by a unanimous vote. (For further details see below.)

EP powers were also significantly extended with amendments to Articles 237 and 238 of the Treaty. This amounts to something of a 'veto' power on issues of EC enlargement, association agreements[44] and international agreements. The EP must give its 'assent', on both occasions, acting 'by an absolute majority of its component members'. Whilst this helps to consolidate the involvement of the EP in the EC's foreign policy,[45] it is, as noted by Richard Corbett, a negative power, in that it gives 'the EP only a chance to accept or reject a package negotiated by others'.[46]

The Commission's powers have been extended under the SEA with the right to initiate legislation in areas such as the environment, research and technological development, and internal market. However, the SEA also stipulates that the Council of Ministers may 'exercise directly implementing powers itself in specific cases'. Yet, by choosing Article 145, under which the powers of the Commission are indirect, the Council of Ministers is obliged, for the first time, to confer power over implementation to the Commission when it is not reserving these powers for itself.[47])

In a subsequent Council of Ministers' decision of 13 July 1987, three types of committees – advisory, management, and regulatory – were introduced to help in the process of implementation. The least intrusive, from the Commission's point of view, is the Advisory Committee, which carries no binding authority over the Commission. On the other hand, if the Commission adopts an implementation procedure contrary to the advice of a Management Committee then the Council of Ministers must be informed. The latter can, within a specified time period, alter the Commission's measures. Failure to comply with this deadline implies that the Commission's measures will be upheld. Finally, the Commission must obtain the approval of a Regulatory Committee before it can adopt any implementation measures. If no approval can be obtained from such a committee, the Council of Ministers will have to decide, within a specified period, whether to adopt the Commission's measures or its own. However, under variant (b) of the Regulatory Committee, the Council can continue to block a decision by a simple majority even when it cannot itself agree to an alternative. The practical implications of the committee procedures, known under the heading of 'comitology', will be explored below.

The institutional provisions of the SEA also tackle another problematic aspect of the decision-making process: voting in the Council of Ministers. The SEA introduces majority voting in five fields of the existing Treaty: Article 28 (alteration of common customs tariff); Article 57(2) (the recognition of qualifications held by self-employed persons); Article 59 (services by nationals of a third country); Article 70(1) (the movement of capital between member states and third countries); and Article 84(2) (provisions for sea and air transport). With regard to new treaty articles qualified voting is introduced in 14 out of the 33 provisions mentioned for voting in the SEA. This

applies in particular to implementing the supplementary R&D programmes (Article 130 K, L, M), and the internal market provisions
(Article 100 A).

The current distribution of weighted votes amongst the member
states[48] ensures that no decision can be taken unless a minimum of
seven member states agree (54 out of the 76 votes). In this way the
'Big Five' can neither force a decision on the rest, nor can the seven
smaller states get a proposal passed without co-operation from at
least one of the larger member states. In December 1986, the Council
revised its own rules of procedure to allow greater use to be made of a
qualified majority at the request of either the Commission or of one
member state supported by a simple majority within the Council.
Two weeks notice must be given in the Council's agenda.

Fiscal policy, the free movement of persons, workers' rights,
immigration measures, measures to combat terrorism and drug
traffic, the trading of illicit antiques and works of art, and monetary
co-operation were exempted from majority voting. Moreover, the
right of 'veto' (Luxembourg compromise), has not been affected by
the SEA.

Dynamics of EC Decision-Making

Four elements of the SEA stand out as far as decision-making is
concerned. These are the extension of majority voting in the Council
of Ministers, the co-operation procedure, comitology, and the EP's
'right of assent'. The 'right of assent', though largely a negative
power, gives the EP the opportunity to participate in EC external
relations. Thus, the EP has more competences in external trade
relations than most national parliaments who generally have only
assent rights on state treaties.[49] To become more positively engaged
in international agreements, it must strengthen the 'Luns–
Westerterp' procedure[50] which aims to keep parliamentary committees informed during the course of negotiations. It must also
influence the Commission's negotiating mandate before negotiations
for an agreement begin. As EC external activities increase, the importance of the 'right of assent' will grow proportionately.

In contrast, the co-operation procedure involves the EP more
immediately and widely. Initially, questions were raised, not the least
by the EP, on whether the co-operation procedure would: (1) allow
the EP to play an effective role in the legislative process of the EC;

and (2) hinder rather than speed-up the EC decision-making process? The answers to these two interrelated questions must be sought in the prevailing SEA provisions, in the way these provisions are applied, and the spirit or extent in which the triangular institutional arrangement is carried out. In examining these aspects, it might be desirable, however, to distinguish between primary, or more immediately apparent effects, and secondary effects. This is being attempted in Table 3.1.

Table 3.1 *Applications of the co-operation procedure*

Primary effects	Secondary effects
1 The number of times the co-operation procedure was invoked;	1 The number of times the legal base for invoking the co-operation procedure was contested either by the EP or the Council and how these issues were resolved;
2 the rate of acceptance by the Commission and Council of EP first reading amendments, and of EP second reading amendments and rejections;	2 the extent to which the Council and the Commission will make information available to the EP as to how the Council arrived at its 'common position';
	3 the ability of the EP to combine effectively the co-operation procedure with the conciliation procedure;
	4 the extent to which Management and Regulatory Committees are involved in the implementation of legislation.

With regard to the legal base, it is in the EP's interest that a broad rather than a narrow interpretation of which issues fall under Article 100A are applied.[51] However, whilst in a few cases the EP, in its first screening, might have convinced the Commission to change to Article 100A, the Council of Ministers can challenge this and revert to the Commission's initial position. Equally, the Commission might want to base its proposals, where appropriate, on articles which require majority voting, like article 100A, in order to speed-up the decision-making process. A case in point was the 1989 proposal for a European Company Statute, which the Council might challenge on the grounds that Article 118, rather than Article 100A, should be applied. The implications over verification of the legal base cannot be fully assessed at this stage, and may require clarification by the Court of Justice.

During the first twenty months of the SEA, the EP, in its first reading, drafted 768 amendments; 72 per cent of which were either partially or totally accepted by the Commission; 42 per cent of the EP's original amendments which were accepted by the Commission appeared in the text of the Council's common positions.[52] Though this is strictly a quantitative assessment and does not reveal the qualitative implications of the amendments in question, the rate of acceptance by both institutions is relatively satisfactory. It is important, however, to stress that these amendments consist of formal and substantive legislative texts, rather than, as was often the case prior to the SEA, declaratory resolutions.[53]

Whilst the first reading lays out the objectives and course of action, it is in the second reading that the EP has to take a strategic decision between accepting or rejecting/amending. If it decides to reject or amend, it must, of course, produce the necessary majority. To obtain an absolute majority, regular attendance by MEPs in 'part sessions' as well as the achievement of a broad consensus are crucial prerequisites. There were initial doubts whether either could be achieved and thus whether the EP would be able to exploit the co-operation procedure fully. These fears have been largely allayed and, according to Neunreither, the EP has met the challenge with 'undoubted success' and produced the necessary majorities in all instances.[54] Undoubtedly, this is a remarkable achievement, considering the diverse nationalities and party political groupings in the EP. It highlights the EP's determination to make a success of this procedure. By changing its internal organisation (rules of procedure and working schedule)[55] monitoring closely the activities in the other two institutions, and by improving its consultation with the other two institutions, the EP has effectively laid the basis for achieving the necessary majorities.

In 1988 the EP, in its second reading, accepted 27 'common positions' and put forward 107 amendments on 23 proposals. The Commission accepted 62 amendments and the Council accepted 19.[56] The EP rejected one proposal which the Council did not over ride because it could not find the necessary unanimity, within the time period specified. As will be shown below, these figures should be considered with caution.

A number of factors determine the EP's action in the second reading. For example, whether the Council has changed the legal base on which a proposal is based; the amount of information available on how the the Council of Ministers arrived at its 'common position'; and whether the EP has recourse to competences elsewhere in the treaty or in inter-institutional agreements. Of considerable importance is the information about how the Council of Ministers arrived at its position, e.g. the extent to which division or cohesion prevails within the Council. Under the co-operation procedure the Council and the Commission are required to inform Parliament. Full information would help to improve the clarity of decision-making and may help to identify potential EP allies within the Council when the second reading takes place there. A working paper of the EP Institutional Committee of April 1989 criticises the Council for giving only 'formal' replies rather than systematic reactions to individual EP amendments. This touches on the subject of confidentiality and is highly sensitive. In short, the Council might be very reluctant to forego such information. The Commission, which might be privy to such delicate information given that it participates in COREPER meetings, is confronted with an awkward choice as to whether or not to divulge such information. On the other hand, the fact that the EP has accepted a majority of 'common positions' might be seen by Council as an indication of the latter's satisfaction with the co-operation procedure.[57]

Under Article 149 paragraph 2b, the Council and the Commission are requested to fully inform the EP the reasons which led the Council to adopt its common position. But in practice this might be difficult to carry out.

There is, however, another way in which the EP has recourse to action. It can invoke the conciliation procedure, on legislation with appreciable financial implications, which was agreed in March 1975.[58] Two areas of the SEA are relevant here: individual research programmes and regional fund decisions. Approaching the issue of consultation from the opposite angle, the EP has tried to prepare an annual legislative programme and timetable. The EP has been able, since 1988, to work out such a programme with the Commission. Corbett sees this as opening 'the door for Parliament to influence the priorities in the Commission's programme and to press for the inclusion of new items (following parliamentary initiative reports) or even the exclusion of items'.[59] However, attempts to extend this agreement to the Council, have so far proven difficult.[60]

Whilst the Commission's right of initiative has been maintained in the SEA, its role as a co-ordinator and arbitrator in the inter-institutional relationship has also been enhanced. The Commission has to weigh up carefully whether to accept or ignore EP amendments in the second reading. As Fitzmaurice points out, 'it has to balance between potential blockage in Council of amendments under the first reading package, or parliamentary criticism, which could even involve the threat of a censure motion'.[61] If it accepts EP amendments, it has to consider that the Council may neither find a majority to accept the Commission's revised proposal nor achieve unanimity to amend it within the time allowed. Therefore, there is a real danger of 'non-decision'.This could also happen if the Commission is faced with a difficult choice on proposals rejected by the EP in the second reading: should it withdraw such proposals or, what is likely to happen, should it let the Council unanimously reinstate its common position and thus secure progress in decision-making. On the other hand, the Commission's acceptance of EP amendments might increase the bargaining position of any state agreeing with the EP. In such situations, according to Fitzmaurice, 'the majority in Council must either "buy off" Parliament or "buy off" its own minority'.[62] In any case, this demonstrates that 'the Council is in fact the Community's senior legislative body' and that the EP's success depends on the Commisssion's support. As Neunreither states: 'it is only when the Commission accepts the wishes expressed by Parliament, in the form of amendments, that these are considered seriously by the Council'.[63] In any case, the confidentiality of Council discussions makes it impossible to assess the degree of Commission support. What disturbs the EP, however, is that the Commission, in an effort to secure a majority vote, modifies adopted EP amendments, by adding 'after discussion with the Council', but fails to discuss these matters with Parliament.[64]

An aspect which has indirect implications for the co-operation procedure, and which particularly involves the Commission, is the form in which Community legislation is implemented. As noted in the EP Graziani report, the comitology procedure 'admittedly rationalises the multitude of procedures that had to be gone through previously, but, in the majority of cases, it allows national officials the possibility of blocking any Commission decision and referring the matter to the Council'.[65] The more Management Committees and Regulatory Committees[66] are introduced into the implementation process, the more the autonomy of the Commission might be affected which, in turn, has implications for the co-operation procedure. The Commission sought further clarification from the Council on the use of such committees. In its Twenty-Second General Report, the Commission notes, however, that:

The simplification of Committee procedures in mid-1987 did not prove to be as effective as expected. The intergovernmental conference's request that priority be given to the 'Advisory Committee' procedure for the completion of the internal market was not followed up. Since the entry into force of the SEA, the Council has adopted this procedure in only five cases; in eleven cases it used delegating procedures which allow the national authorities to block legislation.[67]

The EP challenged the Council on this issue in the Court of Justice in 1988, claiming that the use of Management and Regulatory Committees is contrary to the SEA's intention to strengthen the Commission's executive and management powers and that their use undermines the co-operation procedure. The Court, ruled against the EP because of the procedure for bringing the case forward, not its substance.[68]

In the meantime, the EP has reached an agreement with the Commission whereby the latter will provide full information on all proposals it submits to comitology-type committees. How this will work in practice cannot be fully judged at this stage. However, as noted by Corbett, the Council has not normally accepted EP amendments with regard to Regulatory Committees.[69] Moreover, an additional type of committee has been introduced by Council in July 1987 to provide 'safeguard measures' in the field of trade. The Commission can take directly applicable decisions once it has received the Regulatory Committee's opinion. Nonetheless, under variant 'b' of that procedure these decisions must be approved by the Council within a period of three months, failing which they become null and void.[70] However, under variant 'a' the Commission's decision stands unless the Council of Ministers modifies it within the deadline stipulated.

Assessment of the SEA

What were the major breakthroughs and innovations of the SEA, what are the major drawbacks, and what are the future prospects in policy-making, institutional, and integrative terms?

The SEA represents a pragmatic rather than a strategic attempt to enhance EC integration. It moves EC integration forward in considerable ways but also maintains important national safeguards and derogation possibilities. The proof of the pudding will be in how the SEA provisions will be applied and implemented, and the extent to which exemptions will be requested, accepted or contested. Let us look first at the breakthroughs or innovations.

Progress
The SEA does not represent a grand strategy on how to achieve a political union; this was put forward in the EP Draft Treaty for European Union. Rather, it is a reaction to economic problems and strategies, the complexity of EC decision-making, and domestic and international political developments. From a maximalist point of view, given the degree to which national interests had resurfaced throughout the late 1970s, the SEA represents 'a major act of will and a transformation of the relations between the member states and the way they tackled common problems'.[71] From a minimalist standpoint, it can be argued that in many ways the SEA formalises or legitimises what had already become a Community practice through the intergovernmental method and as such was catching-up with reality.[72] Nonetheless, the fact that it could formalise and legitimise as well as expand the existing Treaties should be heralded as an important achievement, given that it had been unsuccessful in the previous sixteen years.

Overall the SEA strikes a sensible balance between policy objectives and institutional aims. Like other major integrative decisions, it singles out a core sector, namely, the completion of the internal market, as a stepping-stone to further integration. It relates this sector to considerable majority decision-making and to a specific deadline; this has also been attempted before. In a departure from previous practices, it incorporates the EP more effectively in the decision-making process through the co-operation/assent procedures, and makes use of a 'new approach' with regard to the standardisation and harmonisation of policies. Having looked at the co-operation and assent procedures above, a brief discussion will be devoted to the 'new approach' here.

The 'new approach' is derived from the landmark case delivered by the Court of Justice in 1979 known as the Cassis de Dijon Case. The court ruled that if a product had satisfied the standard requirements in one country then it should, in principle, be allowed to be imported into another member state. In view of this judgment, the Commission has decided to modify its harmonisation efforts with the principle of 'mutual recognition'. Basically, this approach allows national standards to be retained but requests member states to accept such standards throughout the Community. In the formulation of legislation, the Commission will set out minimal standards with details to be filled in by EC and national standardisation bodies.[73] This not only has far-reaching implications for the free movement of goods, but also for the free movement of people, in that it applies equally to the 'mutual recognition of qualifications'.[74]

Drawbacks

Whilst the 'new approach' allayed some of the fears member states had about excessive harmonisation or standardisation, and paved the way towards acceptance of both the Commission's White Paper and the SEA's internal market provisions, further measures to protect national interests were deemed necessary. Some of these measures may appear excessive or detrimental to the implementation of the SEA. Among these are the limited use of majority decision making (and by implication the maintenance of the veto); the restraints imposed on the Commission with regard to the implementation of Council decisions (comitology); and the minor concessions made to the EP in EC decision-making, via the co-operation procedure[75] and the right of 'assent'. Most importantly, however, safeguards were introduced in a number of forms in cases where majority voting applies. These involve the 'major needs' clause, the derogation references, and exemptions listed in the Final Act. Article 100 A (paragraph 4) gives permission to member states to apply national provisions on grounds of 'major needs' referred to in Article 36 of the Treaty,'[76] relating to protection of the environment or the working environment'. Under such circumstances, even if out-voted on the actual decision, a member state may refuse admission to imports from other member states. The Court of Justice will probably be involved in deciding when such 'major needs' are justified and when they are not.[77] A similar loophole is created under Article 100 A (paragraph 5) which provides for a 'safeguard clause' and allows a member state to take, in conjunction with Article 36, counterveiling measures subject to a Community control procedure.

On the other hand, safeguard clauses or exemption possibilities do not automatically imply extensive use, or the mere adherence by member states to the minimum standards requested in a certain proposal. Such safeguards introduce a certain amount of flexibility in Council deliberations or in international negotiations and are characteristic of bargaining styles rather than problem solving.[78] This entails difficulties in the evaluation of decisions, for example, it might be misleading to look only at the odd 100 decisions reached by majority voting without considering the way these decisions have been implemented. This also presents difficulties of judicial review by the Court of Justice with regard to, for example, what is meant by measures necessary for 'the working environment' mentioned in Article 118 A (social policy), or those in Article 30(6a) on the meaning of 'political and economic aspects of security' (EPC). Interpretation of the latter is particularly difficult in that Article 30(6c) stipulates that EPC activities have to be compatible with the objectives of the WEU and NATO. In any case, EPC provisions are subject to different interpretations, e.g. whether they are part of the Community legal system or constitute a parallel structure to the Community organisation.[79]

Furthermore, the deadline of 1992 is not legally binding (declaration on Article 8 of the Final Act),[80] and further amendments of the SEA, notably with regard to monetary cooperation, are subject to Article 236, which require unanimity and national ratification. All this may delay the process of the completion of the internal market.

It was these ambiguities which made Pierre Pescatore, a former judge of the Court of Justice, suggest that:

> The Single Act does not contain any tangible commitment by the member states, no obligation which could be defined in precise terms. It opens or seems to open some new avenues, although most of them had already existed under the original E.E.C. Treaty, but each new possibility is outweighed by corresponding loopholes, reservations and new unanimity requirements.[81]

Conclusion

The SEA was an attempt to confront economic stagnation and fragmentation, inefficient EC decision-making, the anticipated consequences of EC enlargement, and domestic and international political changes. The price for those countries who wanted to combine policy reforms with institutional reforms was the insistence by other

countries on inbuilt national safeguards, which might open the
possibility for an EC of two or more tiers.[82] Importantly, there was
an awareness among national governmental actors that unilateral
measures had either failed or proved unproductive, and that additional common and reliable policies were needed. The emerging
governmental consensus, supported by business groups who
expected benefits from a larger and more deregulated market,
embraced largely monetarist and neo-liberal concepts. The SEA thus
resembles a pooling of sovereignties and co-operative federalism, a
phenomenon noted by Wolfgang Wessels,[83] and William Wallace,[84]
and described in Chapters 1 and 2 of this book. Community institutions, in the shape of the Commission, the EP and the Court of
Justice, have been strengthened, but governments have retained
ultimate power over decision-making. This is highlighted in the
preponderant role of the Council of Ministers in EC decision-making
and the array of sub-structures surounding the Council of Ministers,
of which COREPER and the Council Presidency are two important
components. Thus, governments remain the main actors of
integration, attempting to ensure that decision-making is either
retained nationally or shared with central institutions; hence
avoiding a straight transfer of competences from the national to the
Community level. The Council's insistence on Management or
Regulatory Committees (instead of Advisory Committees) in the
implementation process, is indicative of this trend. Nonetheless, the
period of 'entrenched intergovernmentalism'[85] of the 1970s has
given way to a more subtle form of intergovernmentalism in the
1980s, in which there is a more symbiotic decision-making relationship between Community institutions and national governments
than hitherto. Initial fears that the co-operation or assent procedures
would impede the EC decision-making process have so far not
materialised.[86] Not even the much maligned comitology procedure
has resulted in noticeable delays in decision-making. On the other
hand both the co-operation and the assent procedures have
significantly changed the relationship between Council, Commission
and the EP, and improved the EP's role in decision-making. The EP
has moved from a purely consultative role to a limited co-decision-
making role.

Nonetheless, the EP is aware of its limits, especially when
measured against its own draft Treaty for a European Union, and has
called for further institutional reforms. It seeks to strengthen its

legislative capacity in a way which is analogous to its budgetary powers. Whether the EP will succeed in its attempt to achieve either additional formal powers or informal concessions, primarily from the Council of Ministers, will depend on the latter's willingness to concede on either account. It is therefore important to look at the Council or the national dimension and to examine how the Council views the triangular relationship and what improvements, if any, it envisages. Equally, how the Council of Ministers adopts or implements the SEA provisions is of significance to the institutional relationship and the future of the EC. Since much of the Council's role is either affected by, or channelled through, the Council Presidency, it makes sense to concentrate on the role and impact of the Council Presidency. A task which will be pursued in the next two chapters.

Notes

1   Report of the Working Party examining the problems of the enlargement of powers of the European Parliament of the EC, *Bulletin of the European Communities, Supplement* 4/72. This report became known as the 'Vedel Report'.

2   See 'Report on European union', by Leo Tindemans, *Bulletin of the European Communities, Supplement* 1/76.

3   'Report on European institutions', presented to the European Council by the Committee of Three, Brussels, 1979.

4   See, for example, Andrea Boltho, ed., *The European Economy: Growth and Crisis*, Oxford, 1982; M. Albert and R. Ball, 'Towards European economic recovery in the 1980s', report for the European Parliament, 1983; Michael Hodges and William Wallace, eds, *Economic Divergence in the European Community*, London, 1981; Yao-su Hu, *Europe Under Stress*, London, 1981; L. Tsoukalis, ed., *Europe, America and the World Economy*, Oxford, 1986; Peter Flora, ed., *Growth to Limits: The Western European Welfare States since World War II*, IV, Berlin, 1987; and David R. Cameron, 'Sovereign states in a single market: integration and intergovernmentalism in the European Community', paper delivered at the Annual Meeting of the American Political Science Association, San Francisco, 30 August–2 September 1990.

5   For example, social services as a percentage of GNP showed the EC with 17.5 and the USA and Japan with 11.8 and 11.2 respectively in 1986. See 'A Community of twelve: key figures', *European File*, Commission of the EC, March 1989, p. 12.

6   Though there were exceptions like, for example, the British social contract arrangement during the Labour government between 1974 and 1979.

7   E. Damgaard, P. Gerlich and Jeremy Richardson, eds, *The Politics of Economic Crisis: Lessons from Western Europe*, Aldershot, 1989.

8　Comparative unemployment rates (%) were as follows:

	Eur 12	USA	Japan
1975	2.9	8.5	1.9
1981	7.8	7.6	2.2
1985	10.6	7.2	2.6

Source: Europe in Figures, 1988, Office for Official Publications of the European Communities, Luxembourg, p. 13.

9　The penetration of high technology industries (%) was as follows:

	1970	1975	1980
United States	4.8	7.7	14.3
Japan	6.6	6.4	7.9
EC	25.1	32.1	41.1

Source: adapted from Stanley Woods, 'Western Europe: technology and the future', *Atlantic Paper*, no. 63, The Atlantic Institute for International Affairs, London, 1987 p. 35. For further details on the EC technology performance see A. Hertje, ed., *Investing in Europe's Future*, Oxford, 1983; 'Government financing of research and development 1980–1987', *Eurostat*, basic statistics of the Community, Statistical Office of the EC, Luxembourg, 1989; and 'Science and technology indicators II, R&D, invention and competitiveness', OECD, Paris, 1986.

10　Undoubtedly, different countries were affected differently with, for example, the West German economy coming out of the recession much better than some of the other EC countries.

11　See the *Financial Times*, 6 March 1985.

12　Paolo Cecchini with Michel Catinat and Alexis Jacquemin, *The European Challenge 1992. The Benefits of a Single Market*, (English edition by John Robinson), Aldershot, 1988.

13　Ibid., p. 96.

14　Ibid., p. 31.

15　Numerous studies have in the meantime shown the potential economic and consumer benefits of a single market. See, for example, Paolo Cecchini et al., *The European Challenge 1992*; Jacques Pelkmans and Alan Winters with Helen Wallace, Europe's Domestic Market, London, 1988; Tommaso Padoa-Schioppa et al., *Efficiency, Stability and Equity: A Strategy for the Evolution of the Economic System of the European Community*, Oxford, 1987; Michael Emerson et al., *The Economics of 1992*, Oxford, 1988; and 'European economy: the economics of 1992', 35, Commission of the EC, Brussels, March 1988.

16　European Parliament 'Draft treaty establishing the European union', EP Directorate General for Information and Public Relations, Luxembourg, February 1984. For an analysis thereof see Juliet Lodge, 'The Single European Act: towards a new dynamism?', *Journal of Common Market Studies*, XXIV, 3, 1985, pp. 203–223.

17　The Multifibre Agreement (MFA) relates to negotiations between the

EC and developing countries and establishes limits on the growth of textile imports into the EC. For further details see Guido Ashoff, 'The textile policy of the EC', *Journal of Common Market Sudies*, XXII, 1, 1983, pp. 17–46.

18   For a review of the Community's reaction to the 'steel crisis' see Loukas Tsoukalis and Robert Strauss, 'Crisis and adjustment in European steel: beyond laisser-laire', *Journal of Common Market Studies*, XXIII, 3, 1985, pp. 207–28.

19   I am indebted to Richard Corbett for having clarified the distinction to me.

20   Even Britain, not a member of the EMS, had started to align itself voluntarily to the Exchange Rate Mechanism and/or to shadow the German mark.

21   See Fritz Scharpf, 'The joint-decision trap: lessons from German federalism and European integration', *Public Administration*, autumn 1988, pp. 239–78.

22   See Russell J. Dalton, *Citizen Politics in Western Democracies. Public Opinion and Political Parties in the United States, Great Britain, WestGermany, and France*, Chatham, New Jersey, 1988.

23   Peter Schmidt, 'The Franco–German Defence and Security Council', *Aussen Politik* (German foreign affairs journal), XL, 4, 1989, pp. 360–71; and Robert Picht, 'Deutsch-franzoesische Beziehungen nach dem Fall der Mauer: Angst vor "Grossdeutschland"?', *Integration*, 2/90, Bonn, April 1990, pp. 47–58.

24   See 'Solemn Declaration on European Union', *Bulletin of the EC*, no. 6, Commission of the EC, Brussels, 1983, pp. 24–9.

25   More correctly, we are talking about the institutionalisation of policy areas. In many of these areas co-operation had already prevailed via intergovernmental lines. Therefore, the exercise was, in part, to institutionalise policies into the EC Treaty framework which had, already, become Community practice.

26   For example, Greece, Ireland and France stressed the commitment to economic redistribution, the improvement of living standards and the improvement of working conditions. In contrast Britain and West Germany called for greater convergence of the member states economies in order to make the economic environment as similar as possible throughout Europe.

27   See *Europe. Agence Internationale d'Information pour la Presse*, Luxembourg–Bruxelles, no. 4115, 22 June 1985.

28   See Richard Corbett, 'The 1985 intergovernmental conference', in Roy Price, ed., *The Dynamics of European Union*, London, 1987, pp. 255–58; and Otto Schmuck, 'Integrationsschub durch neuen Vertrag? Reformperspektiven im Vorfeld des Mailander Gipfels', *Integration*, 2/85, Bonn, April 1985, pp. 55–67.

29   For a similar conclusion see David Cameron, 'Sovereign states in a single market', and Robert O. Keohane and Stanley Hoffmann, 'European Community politics and institutional change', November 3, 1989, revised version of paper prepared for Florence workshop on the Dynamics of European Integration, 10–12 September, 1989.

30   Robert Putnam, 'Diplomacy and domestic politics: the logic of two-

level games', *International Organization*, XLII, 1988, pp. 427–60; and Robert Putnam, 'The Western Economic Summits: a political interpretation', in Cesare Merlini, ed., *Economic Summits and Western Decision-Making*, London, 1984, pp. 48–9.

31   Ibid.

32   For the official text of the SEA, see the 'Single European Act', *Bulletin of the European Communities, Supplement*, 2/86, Commission of the EC, Office for Official Publications of the EC, Luxembourg, 1986. For a general analysis of the SEA, see H.J. Glaesner, 'The Single European Act', *Year Book of European Law*, VI, Oxford University Press.

33   A second committee set up by the 1984 European Council meeting was on 'a People's Europe', which was chaired by the MEP, Pietro Adonnino. For details of this committee see offprint from the *Bulletin of the European Communities*, 3/85, Office for Official Publications of the EC, Luxembourg, 1985.

34   This decision was taken by 7 votes to 3, with Britain, Denmark and Greece voting against. The brief of the Intergovernmental Conference was to consider the powers of the institutions, the extension of the Community's jurisdiction to new spheres of activity and the establishment of a genuine internal market.

35   Commission of the EC, 'Completing the internal market' (the 'White Paper'), COM (85) 310, Brussels, 14 June, 1985.

36   See note 25 in chapter 1 of this book for further details.

37   See Emil J. Kirchner, *Trade Unions as a Pressure Group in the European Community*, Westmead, 1977, chapter 7.

38   The dates for establishment were: the European Strategic Programme for Research and Information Technology (ESPRIT), 1984; Research in Advanced Communication for Europe (RACE), 1985; Basic Research in Industrial Technologies for Europe (BRITE), 1985; and the European Research Coordination Agency (EUREKA), 1985.

39   This principle is examined in chapter 6 of this book.

40   See T. C. Hartley, *European Community Law*, Oxford, 1983, p. 22.

41   David Edward, 'The impact of the Single Act on the institutions', *Common Market Law Review*, XXIV, 1, 1987, p. 22.

42   These are Article 7 (national discrimination); Article 49 (freedom of movement); Article 54 (freedom of establishment); Article 56 (treatment for nationals of third countries); Article 57 (recognition of diplomas); Articles 100 A and B (internal market measures); Article 118 (health and safety); Articles 130 E (Regional Fund) and 130 O (Community R&D programmes).

43   The salient point is that it is easier for Council to adopt the Commission's re-examined proposal which incorporates Parliament's amendments (needing a qualified majority to do so) than it is to change it (needing unanimity). I am grateful to Richard Corbett for this point.

44   The assent procedure not only applies to basic association agreements but also to any revision or addition to these agreements including financial protocols. See Richard Corbett, 'Testing the new procedures: the European Parliament's first experiences with its new "Single Act" powers', *Journal of Common Market Studies*, XXVII, 4, 1989, p. 359.

45　European Parliament, Directorate General for Research, 'The impact of the European Parliament on Community policies', Research and Documentation Papers: Action Taken Series no. 3, 11–1988, p. 14.

46　Corbett, 'The 1985 intergovernmental conference', p. 262.

47　I am indebted to Richard Corbett for having brought this point to my attention.

48　Under the weighted voting arrangement Britain, France, Italy and West Germany have 10 votes each; Spain has 8, Belgium, Greece, Portugal and the Netherlands have 5 each; Denmark and Ireland have 3 each; and Luxembourg has 2.

49　See Werner Ungerer, 'Die neuen Verfahren nach der Einheitlichen Europaischen Akte: Eine Bilanz aus der Ratsperspektive', *Integration*, 3/89, Bonn, July 1989, pp. 95–106.

50　See William Nicoll, 'Les procedures Luns/Westerterp pour l'information du Parlement europeen', *Revue du Marche Common*, 300, 1986. pp. 475–6.

51　An example where the EP contested the legal base chosen by the Commission concerned the radioactivity of foodstuffs (the Commission choose a legal basis in the EURATOM Treaty instead of Article 100 A). Whilst there are other areas where potential conflict can arise as, for example, on matters concerning the right of workers (where Articles 100 A. 118 A or 235 could be used) both the Commission and the EP have agreed that agricultural research should come under Article 130 H.

52　European Parliament, 'The impact of the European Parliament on Community policies', p. 43.

53　See John Fitzmaurice, 'An analysis of the European Community's co-operation procedure', *Journal of Common Market Studies*, XXVI, 4, 1988, p. 392.

54　See Karl Heinz Neunreither, 'Application of the Single European Act:emergence of a new institutional triangle?', paper presented at the Congress of the International Political Science Association, Washington, August 1988, p. 13.

55　See Emile Noel, *Working Together: The Institutions of the European Community*, Office for Official Publications of the European Communities, Luxembourg, 1988.

56　See Werner Ungerer, 'EC progress under the German Presidency', *Aussen Politik* (German foreign affairs review), XXXIX, 4, 1988, p. 102.

57　Ibid., p. 101.

58　The conciliation procedure was introduced in 1975 to deal with contentious issues (budgetary issues) between the European Parliament, the Commission and the Council of Ministers. For recent developments on this procedure see Michael Shackleton, *Financing the European Community*, 1990.

59　This was the case in the 1990 Commission's programme. A code of conduct was also agreed between the two institutions. I am grateful to Richard Corbett for having brought this point to my attention.

60　Neunreither, 'Application of the Single European Act', p. 15.

61　Fitzmaurice, 'An analysis of the European Community's co-operation procedure', p. 397.

62   Ibid., p. 398.

63   Neunreither, 'Application of the Single European Act', p. 18.

64   See the 'Graziani Report', EP Session Documents, 26 September 1988, pp. 15 and 16.

65   Ibid., p. 13.

66   These committees are not new in EC decision-making. For example, Regulatory Committees were initially used in the management of the Common Custom Tariff, then for the management and adoption of common standards (food, veterinary and plant health regulations), and environmental legislation. See Noel, 'Working together'.

67   See the Twenty-Second General Report on the Activities of the European Communities: 1988, Brussels, 1989, p. 33.

68   The court ruled that the EP is not competent to call for the cancellation of the July 1987 Council decision on 'comitology'.

69   Corbett, 'Testing the new procedures', p. 368.

70   Noel, 'Working together', p. 368.

71   Corbett, 'The 1985 intergovernmental conference' p. 255.

72   For a review of the pre-SEA intergovernmental method, see William Nicoll, 'Paths to European unity', Journal of Common Market Studies, XXIII, 3, 1985, pp. 199–206.

73   Two bodies have been set up at EC-level in this respect: CEN and CENELEX (Comite Europeen de Normalisation (Electrotechnique). For further details see Jacques Pelkmans and Alan Winters, 'Europe's domestic market', pp. 34–7.

74   For further details of the 'new approach', see V. Hirsch, 'Marche interieur: une nouvelle impulsion grace a l'acte unique?', *Revue du Marche Common*, 1987, 303, pp. 1–2.

75   It is important to point out that the Council, by a unanimous vote, can adopt legislative texts that have been rejected by the EP. To avoid such situations the EP requested the Commission to withdraw from the Council any proposal rejected by the EP. The EP aim is also to ensure 'democratic control' over EC decision-making.

76   Article 36 of the Treaty allows restrictions on the import or export of goods on certain grounds such as: public morality, public policy or public security; the protection of health and life of humans, animals or plants; the protection of national treasures possessing artistic, historic or archeological value; or the protection of industrial and commercial property.

77   To contest such cases, any member state or the Commission can challenge the validity of the claim in the Court of Justice. This is itself an innovation in that formerly, under Article 169 and 170 of the treaties, only the Commission, through its 'reasoned opinion', performed the initial screening of requests for derogations, and follow-up proceedings with the Court of Justice.

78   See Scharpf, 'The joint-decision trap'.

79   See 'Graziani report', p. 11.

80   For further clarifications see note 25 in chapter 1 of this book.

81   Pierre Pescatore, 'Some critical remarks on the "Single European

Act" ', *Common Market Law Review*, 1, 1987, p. 15.

82   For an analysis of a 'two' or 'multi-tier' EC development see Helen Wallace with Adam Ridley, *Europe: The Challenge of Diversity*, London, 1985; and Eberhard Grabitz, ed., *Abgestufte Integration: eine Alternative zum herkoemlichen Integrationskonzept*, Kehl am Rhein, 1984.

83   Wolfgang Wessels, 'The growth of the EC system – A product of the dynamics of modern European states? A plea for a more comprehensive approach', paper delivered at the XIVth World Congress of the International Political Science Association, 28 August to 1 September, Washington DC, 1988.

84   William Wallace, 'Less than a federation, more than a regime: the Community as a political system', Helen Wallace, William Wallace and Carole Webb, eds, *Policy Making in the European Community*, 2nd edition, 1983, pp. 403–36.

85   See Paul Taylor, *The Limits of European Integration*, London, 1983.

86   The EP, in its Internal Regulation (Articles 39 and 40), has reserved the option to delay giving an opinion in its first reading. If, after debate, the Commission's position does not meet the Parliament's demands, Parliament may decide to refer the matter back to Committee for two months. For further details see EP, 'Impact of the European Parliament on Community policies', p. 7.

4

The evolving role of the Council Presidency

Introduction

The Council Presidency can be described as a body which has grown in status more by default than by design. With neither the Paris nor the Rome Treaties providing any substantial base, the role of the Council Presidency was shaped largely by a number of important events in EC history such as the Luxembourg compromise of 1966, and EPC, Technical Councils and European Councils of the 1970s. Overall, the emergence of the Council of Ministers after 1966 coincided with a decline in the role of the Commission and reflected attempts by member states to control the scope, level and pace of integration. The need for greater involvement by both COREPER and the Council Presidency grew as pressure mounted for EC governments to meet both the economic crisis and the international monetary disorder and as governments sought to maintain national control over EC matters. Thus, changes in the international environment, institutional inadequacies, the increased volume of Community activities, the technicalities of harmonisation and standardisation, and growth of member states from, six to twelve are the main reasons for the Council Presidency playing a greater role in EC affairs.[1]

To judge the importance of the Council Presidency in EC decision-making necessitates a review of the main functions it has accrued over time, the way it co-operates with other EC institutions and the constraints under which it operates. It is the task of this chapter to explore how the Presidency came to assume an important role, what its main tasks are, and which factors either hinder or promote its effectiveness. Subsequent chapters will then deal with a comparison of different working methods employed by Council Presidencies, their overall achievements, and their future prospects.

Evolution of the Council Presidency

The EC treaties only endowed the Council Presidency with modest powers. Indeed, most of the initial powers derived from the 1958 Council standing orders which assigned to the Presidency: (1) the chairmanship of COREPER; (2) the management of agenda-setting and minute-taking in COREPER and Council of Ministers' meetings; (3) the signing of documents and notifying of decisions, and (4) the representation of the Council of Ministers in the EP. All these tasks were to be carried out in close collaboration with the General Secretariat of the Council of Ministers.

The first boost to the Council Presidency's responsibility occurred as a consequence of the 1965–6 EC constitutional crisis which reinforced the element of national control over, and interest in, EC decision-making. Whilst the Commission took a battering from the impact of the Luxembourg compromise and, for a long time, played a subservient role to the Council of Ministers, the latter, in turn, found itself confronted with a seemingly unsolvable task of working-out compromises among EC members. As shown in chapter 3, changes in the international environment in the 1970s, such as the rise of OPEC, trade disputes and monetary disorder, tended to exacerbate differences in national interests. As the competition between national interests became more overt, a division of labour within the Council of Ministers was eventually attempted to cope with the increasing backlog of unresolved Community business. The General Affairs Council, consisting of foreign ministers, became a forum for overall co-ordination for Council of Ministers' affairs and institutional development. Technical Councils, like the Council of Agriculture Ministers, deal with specific policy areas. However, neither the General Affairs Council nor the Technical Councils were able to improve decision-making sufficiently and problems were pushed up to the level of Heads of Government and State (the European Council) and towards a more active involvement of the six-monthly Council Presidency.

In this second wave of acquired Presidency responsibilities two aspects stand out in particular: the European Council and European Political Cooperation (EPC). The European Council, established in 1975, represented an attempt to increase the decision-making capabilities of the Community and to institutionalise the participation of top-level national political decision-makers in the EC decision-making process.[2] EPC, established in 1970, has become a means whereby EC foreign ministers meet to discuss the co-ordination of foreign policy.[3] Both initiatives signify the intergovernmental method as the guiding mechanism of EC co-operation. However, whilst the intergovernmental method could effectively sideline the Commission in EC decision-making, it required a replacement for the Commission's role. The Council Presidency became this replacement and the sole forum through which Council of Ministers' activities were initiated, co-ordinated and represented. This is particularly noticeable with regard to EPC. As pointed out by Bassompierre, the much lighter EPC institutional structure and the nature of its purpose – deprived of the legislative and regulatory powers of the EC and largley limited to the consideration of policies and hammering out of policy statements – have made it totally dependent on the Presidency.[4] Moreover, because of the autonomous gestation of EPC, 'the European Council is the "crowning touch" in the Presidency's attempt to link EC activities with those of EPC'.[5]

Commentators usually agree that no institution has influenced Community and Western European policies in the 1970s and early 1980s more than the European Council.[6] The preparation, agenda-setting and drafting of compromise solutions of the European Council is largely the task of the Presidency, and greatly involves the foreign minister of the Presidency. This gives the Presidency significant influence on the course of the European Council.[7] It is for this reason that the role of the Presidency was subject to various reform efforts between 1975 and 1983 (Tindemans' Report, Report of the Three Wise Men, and EPC reports of Luxembourg, Copenhagen and London)[8] It is therefore not surprising that both the European Council and the Council Presidency are mentioned in the Single European Act (SEA).

What then does the Council Presidency actually do and how can its role be assessed? In the following, we will look first at its structure and at its tasks, and later consider factors which affect its role.

Structure and functions of the Council Presidency

Structure of the Presidency
The Council Presidency rotates in alphabetical order every six months among the member states.[9] It is carried out at the levels of:

the European Council; the Council of Ministers, COREPER; Working Groups; and embassies in 'third' countries. At the European Councils it is the head of government or state of the country holding the six-monthly presidency who acts as the host and chairs the meeting. At Council of Ministers level, where legislation is being decided, European Council decisions being followed up, and the most important activities during the Presidency are being co-ordinated, it is the foreign minister of the Presidency who plays a leading role. To understand this role we have to examine both the different Council structures and the relevance of these Councils.

Three types of Council of Ministers can be distinguished according to the frequency of their meetings and their political weight.[10] First and foremost is the General Affairs Council, consisting of foreign ministers, which meets nearly every month and deals with major policy issues of European integration and foreign relations. Importantly, it co-ordinates the activities of the other Councils (Technical Councils), provides a link between Community and EPC issues, and prepares the European Council. It therefore assumes a certain political pre-eminence. The General Affairs Council meets mostly in the form of plenary sessions, e.g. each country having around ten delegates present, and occasionally in the form of restricted sessions with a smaller number of delegates from each country. A distinction should be made between General Affairs Councils and Councils dealing with European Political Co-operation. The latter also involve the foreign ministers, but their decisions on EPC matters do not carry any legislative effect.[11] Though there are, on average, four formal meetings and two informal EPC meetings annually, there is some overlap with discussions in the General Affairs Council. A second type involves the Economic and Financial Council (ECOFIN), and the Agricultural Council and regroups the respective finance (sometimes accompanied by the economics ministers) and agricultural ministers. Each Council meets nearly every month. Other Councils make up the third category, which can be further sub-divided into those which deal with issues in which the EC has some degree of competence, (like budget, internal market, environment, research and development, social affairs, development aid), and those involving areas in which member states aim to co-ordinate their different policies, such as education. Some of these meet ten times a year (internal market council) and others only twice (budget council), but the task for the Presidency is the same. Details on the frequency of Council of Ministers' meetings are provided in Table 4.1.

Preparation for Council of Ministers' sessions is done mainly by the Committee of Permanent Representatives, commonly known by its French abbreviation of COREPER. Exceptions apply to agriculture and ECOFIN Councils as well as to EPC matters. In the case of ECOFIN Councils, the Monetary Committee, consisting of senior civil servants from the finance ministries, advise the finance ministers directly without having to refer to COREPER. The Special Agricultural Committee is substituted for COREPER in the Council of Agricultural Ministers. Because of the financial and political implications, however, COREPER does handle the more politically sensitive issues.[12] With regard to EPC matters, the Political Committee takes on the administrative and management task of COREPER.

COREPER developed primarily after the 1966 Luxembourg compromise and its vast array of duties as well as its importance has

Table 4.1 *Frequency of Council of Ministers' meetings, 1985–89*

	1985	1986	1987	1988	1989
Foreign Affairs	14	11	14	14	13
Agriculture	14	11	14	12	12
Internal Market	3	7	6	8	10
ECOFIN	7	9	8	6	8
Research	2	4	3	4	5
Social Affairs	2	2	2	2	5
Environment	3	3	4	3	4
Fisheries	3	5	3	5	4
Transport	3	4	4	4	4
Industry	6	6	5	2	4
Education	1	2	1	2	3
Telecommunications	–	–	–	1	3
Budget	5	5	6	4	2
Consumer Affairs	1	2	3	–	2
Health	–	1	1	2	2
Aid and Development	2	2	2	2	2
Energy	3	3	3	2	2
Others	2	2	2	3	2
Total	71	79	81	76	87

Source: Information obtained from the General Secretariat of the Council of Ministers.

grown with the development of Community activities. It is comprised of the member states ambassadors to the Community, known as permanent representatives, and their staffs; approximately 100 per delegation for the larger countries.[13] COREPER negotiates on the Commission's proposal and tries either to deal with, or to identify, the technical, economic or political difficulties which need to be resolved in order for a decision to be reached. The Presidency will have to decide whether to involve working groups in the discussions or whether to keep discussions at COREPER level. Although they are national civil servants who follow national instructions, it is possible, as suggested by Troy Johnston, for these representatives 'to adopt a larger frame of reference than their own countries' needs or at least to understand the requirements of satisfying twelve national interests and the additional interest of the Community, as represented by the Commission'.[14] In many cases, therefore, COREPER is able to reach compromises which enables it to produce a text ready for ministerial approval. These are known as the 'A points' on the Council of Minister's agenda; which are distinct from 'B points' on which ministers are asked to hold further discussions and negotiations at Council of Ministers' level. COREPER thus acts as a 'clearing house' for proposals coming from the Commission by signalling the degree of support, the extent of the problem or the amount of preparation needed to deal with the Commission proposal.[15]

COREPER comprises two distinct meetings, namely, COREPER I, consisting of the deputy permanent representatives – dealing with technical matters, but also the budget – and COREPER II, in which the permanent representatives meet and in which the more important decisions are taken. The former usually meets every Wednesday, and the latter every Thursday. A further division of labour involves the Antici Group (named after the Permanent Italian Representative who initiated it in 1975) which precedes COREPER meetings and deals with the preparation of the European Council. It facilitates the flow of information between the Presidency, the Council Secretariat, the Commission and the member governments.[16] COREPER, in conjunction with the Presidency, co-ordinates the various working groups. However, COREPER's influence has not progressed evenly with Community developments. For example, European Councils, by excluding COREPER from its meetings, restrict COREPER to a more limited role than is the case in Council of Ministers' affairs.[17]

European Councils occasionally involve ad hoc committees as well, such as the Institutional Committee, and the European People's Committee (in 1984–5), which carry out work COREPER may otherwise perform.[18] Similarly, with the establishment of EPC in 1970, COREPER has been displaced by the Political Committee which acts independently of COREPER and meets about twenty times a year. It is assisted by the European correspondents, who meet monthly and ensure that EPC functions smoothly inside the national foreign ministries. They also run a telex network, known as COREU, which handles around six thousand telexes annually. In addition, reference was made above to the absence of COREPER in ECOFIN Councils and its limited role in Agricultural Councils.

In both COREPER and EPC there are working groups. On EPC matters the various working groups (covering either geographic regions or such issues as the UN, CSCE conferences, disarmament, human rights, terrorism, etc.) receive a mandate from the Political Committee of EPC and report to it. There are approximately two hundred working groups under COREPER and approximately twenty-five working groups under EPC.

The General Secretariat of the Council of Ministers is, as Bonvicini and Regelsberger point out, perhaps the least known of the Community bodies, but it is the one which has gained the most prestige since the establishment of the European Council.[19] Three main features can be attributed to the General Secretariat: a conference centre, an administrative clearing house, and an advisor to the Presidency.[20] In its capacity as a conference centre, the General Secretariat carries out logistical tasks, like the translation, preparation and distribution of documents, organisation of rooms, the interpretation services, and security measures for Council of Minsters' or European Council meetings. With regard to the administrative clearing house, the General Secretariat takes minutes at various Council-level meetings, prepares drafts, and gives legal advice. It also ensures that delegations have the opinions of the EP and the Economic and Social Committee, as soon as they have been issued. As a permanent fixture, unlike the Presidency, its cumulative experience can make it a valued consultant and thus an important advisor of the Presidency. In this respect the Secretariat may have an effect on political outcomes: e.g. in the drafting of presidential compromise proposals, it can provide 'nuanced tilts of wording if so desired by the Presidency'.[21] Since the arrival of Ersboll as Secretary

General, the General Secretariat has changed from a purely passive to a more active role in the drawing up of compromises. In conjunction with the Presidency's programme, the General Secretariat advises on the number and type (informal or formal) of meetings required and on the timing of preparatory meetings at COREPER and expert levels. Together with the Presidency, it engages in a method of indicative planning. There is thus constant consultation between the Presidency and the General Secretariat levels about objectives, strategies and technicalities. Nonetheless, the extent to which the General Secretariat is used varies among Presidencies; smaller countries usually depend more heavily on the Sectretariat. However, the Secretariat must never appear to interfere with the Presidency's work. The size of the General Secretariat has grown steadily and compromises the Secretary General and a total staff of about two thousand.

The role of the Secretary General deserves a special mention. The Secretary General is particularly closely involved in the preparation of European Council meetings. This involves the preparation of; preliminary documents and drafts for the Presidency, a draft letter sent by the President of the European Council to his/her colleagues outlining the programme of discussions for the European Council (effectively the agenda) and a 'speaking note' for use by the President of the European Council. The Secretary General also participates closely in the drafting and finalising of the communique of the European Council.[22]

As with COREPER, EPC matters are run by the EPC Secretariat, which was established through the SEA, and which assists the Presidency in preparing and implementing the activities of EPC. Unlike the General Secretariat of the Council of Ministers, however, it has no budget of its own and operates only with a small staff of about twenty. It contains several national diplomats who are seconded for two years by their respective foreign ministries. They begin their service prior to their country holding the six-monthly Presidency, and end just after.[23]

Table 4.2 summarises, in a simplified way, the main structures in which the Council Presidency plays a role. It should be noted that this table does not include all the roles of a Presidency. For example, the Presidency also co-ordinates EC activities in 'third' countries' embasssies, e.g. the Soviet Union. They also organise, where necessary, working groups. What the table helps to demonstrate, however, is the heavy workload Presidencies encounter in the form of a multitude of meetings at various Council level; often several meetings occur on a given working day. Having examined the structure in which the Presidency operates, let us now look at the functions of the Presidency.

Table 4.2 *Council structure*

Level of participants	Type of forum	Frequency of meetings
Prime Ministerial	European Council	Twice a year
	Gen. Aff. Council	Monthly
Ministerial	Council of Ministers	
	Technical councils	Mon. to ann.
	I	Weekly
Top ranking	COREPER	
National Civil	II	Weekly
Service	Pol. Committee for EPC	20 times ann.
	Agriculture	Monthly
	Specialised committees	
	Finance	Twice a year
National Civil	COREPER working groups	Mon. to ann.
Service generally	working groups	Mon. to ann.
	EPC	
	Correspondent group	Monthly
Community Civil	Gen. Secretariat of the	
Service dealing	Council of Ministers	Permanently
with Council of		
Ministers' Affairs	EPC Secretariat	Permanently

Functions of the Presidency

Four main functions of the Council Presidency can be identified. These are the administrative, initiative, co-ordination, and representational functions.[24] There is a certain amount of overlap between these, but for analytical purposes each function will be treated separately.

The administrative function. As Wallace and Edwards point out, the management of Council business is the least glamorous but most important function of the Presidency.[25] Even though, as mentioned above, a distinction should be made between EC affairs generally and EPC matters, the Presidency has to deal with both. The administrative function involves the organisation of meetings, the preparation of decisions as well as the implementation of EPC decisions. On the input side of decisions, the Presidency is responsible for the timetable of meetings at working-group level, COREPER, Council of Ministers' and European Council level, and for the minutes/conclusions of these meetings. There are around 150 working groups (both COREPER and EPC) in operation during any given Presidency. The Presidency also gives a press conference at the end of European Council meetings ('conclusions of the Presidency'). However, neither the 'conclusions of the Presidency' nor other official statements are legal acts.[26] This all requires great organisational resources, skill and familiarity with EC procedures. The technical and legal assistance provided by the General Secretariat of the Council is invaluable here. On the output side, the Presidency is responsible for the correct and efficient implementation of EPC decisions. In this respect, it strays into the Commission's role, assigned by the treaties, of ensuring that EC decisions are implemented correctly.

The initiative function.   With regard to the initiative function, the Presidency once again collides with a traditional Commission function. However, it must be pointed out that the Presidency's initiatives have no corresponding legal powers to those of the Commission either in the input phase or in implementation of EC decision-making.[27] In any case Presidency initiatives, other than EPC ones, will have to go through the official stage of Commission proposals before they can be put on the Council of Ministers' desk for a decision. In practice, however, there is a great deal of collaboration between the Presidency and the Commission in the setting of the six-monthly priorities. The exception, once again, are EPC matters where the influence of the Commission, because of the inter-governmental method involved in EPC, is much more limited. The six-monthly programme of priorities, which the Presidency has been required to produce since the inception of the European Council in 1975, gives it an opportunity to make an impact, especially if it receives both support from the Commission, the EP and member governments. The impact will also depend on the extent to which the Presidency seeks to pursue and balance national objectives with Community policies. In any case, before we can turn to this question, which will be dealt with in chapter 5, we need to consider the Presidency's ability to co-ordinate diverse national interests, to act as a broker or mediator and to liaise effectively with the Commission and the EP in the pursuit of its priorities.

The co-ordination function. Efficient management of Council business and skill in stimulating consensus contribute to the pace and quality of decision-making.[28] In this mediating and finalising role the Presidency needs to be familiar with the relevant issues. At the various levels in which the Presidency is engaged, it must play the mediatory role of the chairman. It must recognise when to expedite and when to delay negotiations on certain issues. With regard to European Councils, it acts as a filter for all communications, and plays a leading role in consensus building or compromise formulations.[29] Effective co-ordination of Council affairs also involves constructive liaison with the Commission and the EP. This is facilitated by regular meetings between the President of COREPER and the Commission, who together discuss the agenda of both COREPER and the Council of Ministers. Moreover, in the last few years, it has become customary for the Presidency, consisting of several ministers, to meet the whole Commission at the beginning of its term. With regard to the EP, the Presidency, in the person of the foreign minister, presents the programme of policy priorities to the EP, and, if not upstaged by a head of government or state, gives an account of its achievements at the end of the Presidency. These high-level contacts also enable the Commission and the EP (especially through links with the EP Political Committee) to have an input into EPC issues. There is no doubt that such contacts impose a heavy commitment in terms of time. In addition, the Presidency might view the Commission and EP not only as partners but also as rivals. Therefore, as Bonvicini and Regelsberger suggest, 'the degree of participation of each individual institution and the importance that is given to its suggestions largely depend on the presidency-in-office'.[30]

The representational role. The Presidency carries out a dual representational role. One involves representing the Council's position at the Commission and the EP, and the other relates to the Community's position vis-a-vis third countries, especially on EPC issues. For example, with regard to the co-operation procedure, it must communicate to the EP the 'common position' taken by the Council. In external matters, the Presidency has, for example, acted and signed on behalf of the member states in the preceedings of the 1975

Helsinki Act, e.g. sharing with the Commission in EC affairs, but acting alone in EPC matters. Table 4.3 highlights the main functions of the Council Presidency and some of the specific tasks they entail.

Table 4.3 *Functions and tasks of the Council Presidency*

Functions	Specific tasks
Administrative	– Screen Commission's proposals.
	– Organise working groups, meetings, documents, minutes and draft conclusions.
	– Implement EPC decisions.
Initiative	– Set six-monthly programme of policy priorities.
	– Initiate EPC issues.
Co-ordination	– Mediate in negotiations at working group, COREPER, Council of Ministers and European Council level, and strive for a 'finalising role'.
	– Liaise with the Commission and the EP on agenda-setting and proposals for compromise solutions.
Representational	– Represent the Council's stand at the Commission or the EP.
	– Represent the Community's position vis-a-vis third countries, especially on EPC matters.

Determinants of Presidency's effectiveness

Having looked at functions, attention will now turn to the influence of the Presidency in EC decision-making, by identifying some of the factors which either help or hinder the role of the Presidency.

Time factor. With only six months available, the Presidency's period is 'barely longer than the learning curve'.[31] This is why decisions are bunched at the end of June and December and represent a blitzktieg-like finish. The assistance of both the General Secretariat and the EPC Secretariat, and advanced planning (usually a year in advance)[32] counteract some of the shortcomings associated with such a brief period in office and also provide an element of continuity in the office of the Presidency. A similar service was extended on EPC matters through the 'Troika' system,[33] which preceded the establishment of the EPC Secretariat. Nonetheless, planning is difficult for a variety of reasons.

Among the issues in which the Presidency gets involved during a six-monthly period there are some which can be anticipated or for which preparations can be made in advance. The arrival of Portugal and Spain as new members in 1986, the EC anniversary in 1987, the court case in 1986, (initiated by the EP, over the Council of Ministers' failure to introduce a common transport policy),[34] and the renewal of the Lome Convention fall into this category. Even the fact of whether a Presidency holds the first or second six months of the year has certain bearing on the planning, in that agricultural prices have to be agreed in the first half and the budget in the second half of the year. On the other hand, the Chernobyl nuclear accident of May 1986 was an unforeseen issue to which the Presidency had to react instantly.

However, how a Presidency handles both foreseen and unforeseen issues depends on a number of factors such as experience, commitment, size of the country, and collaboration with other EC institutions.

Experience at both ministerial and civil servant level.   As suggested by Troy Johnston, the Presidency 'must have precise knowledge of EC procedures and issue areas, an understanding of the motives behind countries' bargaining positions and a large storehouse of political finesse'.[35] Whilst on procedural questions the Presidency can rely to a large extent on the knowledge of the two Council secretariats, it must make its own effort to come to grips with the motives and bargaining positions of other member states. The length and the continuity of experience, held at either the ministerial or civil service level, is an important factor in the way such an effort can be carried out, and highlights certain difficulties for members such as Portugal and Spain[36] who have recently entered the EC. This also relates to styles and methods of how the 'good office' is to be used, e.g. the appropriate time to call for a vote, or the timing and framing of compromise solutions and package deals. Experience may also relates to size.

Size factor.   Different advantages and disadvantages may arise in connection with the size of a country. There is no doubt that the sheer adminstrative task of a Presidency places a heavy burden on the small member states, especially Luxembourg. Yet it can be argued that because information and communication is confined to a relatively small segment of people, a more effective handling of the task in hand might be secured. Moreover, small countries may act as a broker and mediator when 'big' countries hold opposing views. On the other hand, the clout of large countries might be needed to launch major initiatives or to untie major deadlocks.[37] A not altogether unrelated issue can be the extent to which a Presidency is prepared to make concessions on questions of national interest and how salient such a concession is in the context of EC decision making. This in turn poses the question of commitment.

Commitment. Commitment to the goals of integration may affect the degree to which a Presidency is prepared to pursue Community objectives. This may be connected with either the introduction of symbols, like the issuing of ECUs as legal tender (Belgium 1987) or entry into the EMS (Spain 1989), or an extensive campaigning (the touring of capitals of EC member states, letter writing to heads of government or states, etc.). As with other issues, commitment rests on cohesion within a government. Coalition governments might find this more difficult to achieve than single-party governments. On the other hand, the West German ministerial autonomy[38] might allow ministers to express greater commitment to integration than is the case in Britain where the Prime Minister exercises considerable authority over Community matters. In addition, the special relationship between the Danish government and the Danish Parliamentary 'Market' Committee on EC issues has a bearing on outcomes.[39]

Collaboration with Commission and EP. Most Presidencies engage in extensive co-operation with the Commission and according to Bassompierre 'the best results have been achieved by good teamwork with the Commission'.[40] The opposite practice consists of multiple bilateralism, mainly between the Presidency and representatives of other member states at top political level. These informal contacts tend to exclude or, at least reduce, the role of the Commission.[41]

With regard to the EP, mention must be made of inter-institutional co-operation. This involves meetings: (1) between the presidents of the Council, Commission, and the Parliament; (2) at the level of parliamentary committees – to discuss the take-up of parliamentary amendments to legislative proposals still being considered by Council as well as four meetings with the Political Affairs Committee of the EP; (3) at the administrative level, where, among others, an inter-institutional computerised information network is being planned to establish a common data base. Other links between the EP and the Presidency consist of the statements made by the President-in-office before the EP at the beginning and at the end of the six-monthly period. Equally, ministers, not just the foreign ministers, reply to oral questions in EP plenary sessions or have discussions with representatives of EP committees. Finally, ministers reply to written questions posed by MEPs.

The Commission participates fully in EPC meetings and carries, with the Presidency, the responsibility for consistency between EPC and the Commission's external policy. Article 30(4) of the SEA instructs the Presidency to inform the EP on EPC and to ensure that its views are taken into account.

So far the impression might have arisen that the effectiveness of the Presidency relates primarily to experience and commitment. However, we have to remember that outside support and external circumstances are equally important. It is, therefore, important to pay attention to the general economic and political climate. Since chapter 5 will deal with this aspect more thoroughly, only a few points will be raised in the following.

National general elections may occur during a Presidency but are more likely to take place in other member states. A by-product of elections can be an undue prominence of the national interest. An absence of elections, on the other hand, can mean more freedom from domestic constraints and an ability to pay more attention and energy to EC affairs. But a number of qualifications have to be made with regard to elections. Though the extent of uncertainty might be the same, different implications might arise between pre- and post-election periods. In pre-election periods, governments, especially those consisting of coalitions, manifest considerable reluctance to engage or commit the country to major EC policy matters or reforms for fear of upsetting public opinion. Equally, certain countries might be hamstrung in EC affairs because of problems over forming a coalition government and thus have to act through a caretaker government. Although this situation might affect certain countries more than others, such as Italy and the Netherlands, the period of 'cohabitation' in France (1986 to 1988) had similar implications. This leads to a consideration of the country or countries in which elections occur, e. g. small or large ones and the number of elections taking place during a given Presidency. In addition, it is important to establish which type of election is involved: a general, state or presidential election, or a referendum. Finally, cabinet reshuffles need to be assessed since they affect the continuity and style of Council of Ministers' work. As Putnam explains, 'if frequent changes are made in the holders of cabinet office then decisions will be reached through political skill rather than through expertise'.[42] On the other hand, the impact of elections and cabinet reshuffles must be related to the extent to which cross-party consensus prevails on EC matters within a given country.

Preliminary assessment of Council Presidency

The Presidency represents an opportunity to either raise the profile of a country, government or leader, or to make a significant political impact on Community policies. But there are also risks that expectations cannot be fulfilled within the limited time available, or that other member states and EC institutions will be antagonised by the conduct of the Presidency. A distinction should be made between the skill and innovation a Presidency might bring to bear and the economic and political influences which might affect its work. With regard to skill and innovation, a Presidency might be assessed through:

1 the managerial skill, smooth running of meetings, or innovative working methods;
2 the selection of policy priorities, e.g. priorities which receive broad support from other member states and EC institutions, and/or which involve significant concessions by the country holding the Presidency;
3 the practice of 'good' office, e.g. the degree to which it is seen as an honest broker, mediator, or coalition builder;
4 the extent and way in which difficult issues were tackled , e.g. the phasing-in of the SEA;
5 the 'presidential' style in which the objectives were represented to the other EC institutions and the reputation of the Community was promoted with respect to 'third' countries.

In general terms, the Council Presidency entails limited, though definite, opportunities in policy making and leadership terms. Whilst the Presidency might be more limited to get its way on policy initiatives, it has greater leeway in blocking issues by either keeping them off the agenda or by delaying their decisions at working group or COREPER/Political Committee level. There is also the chance for the Presidency to educate and inform domestic opinion on EC issues and the Community record.[43]

Conclusion

The Council Presidency has experienced considerable emancipation since 1958. External influences, such as the arrival of EPC, Technical Councils and European Councils, became the main catalysts of this process, rather than internal dynamics. The desire to maintain national control over EC decision-making and to respond to economic and international problems are underlying motives for this. As a consequence, the Presidency plays an increasingly central role as a manager, initiator, and co-ordinator (consensus-broker) of EC affairs. Besides this role, the Council Presidency provides each member state, regardless of size, experience or commitment, with both the opportunity and responsibility to define the Community agenda and to share in the success and failures of Community policies both internally and externally.

It is the task of the following chapter to explore how this opportunity and responsibility is met in eight empirical cases and what lessons can be drawn from it.

Notes

1   See for example, Helen Wallace and Geoffrey Edwards, 'European Community: the evolving role of the Presidency of the Council,' *International Affairs*, October 1976, pp. 535–50; Colm O Nuallain, ed., in collaboration with Jean-Marc Hoscheit, *The Presidency of the European Council of Ministers. Impacts and Implications for National Governments*, London, 1985; Simon Bulmer and Wolfgang Wessels, *The European Council: Decision-Making in European Politics*, London 1987; Guy de Bassompierre, *Changing the Guard in Brussels: An Insider's View of the EC Presidency*, New York, 1988.

2   See Jean-Marc Hoscheit, 'The European Council and domestic policy making', Jean-Marc Hoscheit and Wolfgang Wessels, eds, *The European Council 1974–1986: Evaluation and Prospects*, Maastricht, 1988, p. 92.

3   See Roy H. Ginsberg, *Foreign Policy Actions of the European Com-*

munity. The Politics of Scale, London, 1989; and Alfred Pijpers, Elfriede
Regelsberger and Wolfgang Wessels, eds, in collaboration with Geoffrey
Edwards, *European Political Cooperation in the 1980s: a Common Foreign
Policy for Western Europe*, Dordrecht, 1988.

4   de Bassompierre, *Changing the Guard in Brussels*, p. 121.

5   Ibid.

6   See for example, Wolfgang Wessels, 'The European Council: a
denaturing of the Community or indispensable decision-making body?', in
Hoscheit and Wessels, eds, *The European Council 1974–1986*, p. 7; and
Bulmer and Wessels, *The European Council*.

7   Mary Troy Johnston, 'The European Council: and integrative or
disintegrative innovation?', paper presented at the Community Studies
Association inaugural conference, Washington DC, May 1989, p. 23.

8   Axel Vornbaumen, *Dynamik in der Zwangsjacke. Die
Praesidentschaft im Ministerrat der Europaeischen Gemeinschaft als
Fuehrungsinstrument*, Bonn, 1985, pp. 29–30.

9   The sequence until the end of 1992 is Belgium, Denmark, Germany,
Greece, Spain, France, Ireland, Italy, Luxembourg, Portugal, the Netherlands, and the United Kingdom. This sequence corresponds to the country
names in alphabetical order in their native tongue.

10   de Bassompierre, 1988, *Changing the Guard in Brussels*, p. 21.

11   Article 31 of the SEA makes it clear that EPC is not a part of the EC
and that the powers of the court can not be exercised in the case of EPC.

12   de Bassompierre, 1988, *Changing the Guard in Brussels*, p. 43.

13   The size of permanent delegations is affected by the country's prox-
imity to Brussels, e.g. France has considerably larger staff than Spain. For
further details see Fiona Hayes-Renshaw, Christian Laquesne and Pedro
Mayor-Lopez, 'The permanent representation of the member states of the
European Community', *Journal of Common Market Studies*, XXVIII, 2,
1989, pp. 119–37.

14   Troy Johnston, 'The European Council', p. 15.

15   Gianni Bonvicini and Elfriede Regelsberger, 'The decision-making
process in the EC's European Council', *The International Spectator*, XXII,
3, July–September 1987, p.166.

16   Troy Johnston, 'The European Council', p. 12.

17   Bonvicini and Regelsberger, 'The decision-making process', p. 166.

18   See Bulmer and Wessels, 1987, *The European Council*, p. 108.

19   Bonvicini and Regelsberger, 'The decision-making process', p. 164.

20   I am indebted to William Nicol for having brought these distinctive
features to my attention.

21   Troy Johnston, 'The European Council', p. 9.

22   The European Council communique is usually prepared by the head
of the Permanent Delegation of the Presidency, a representative of the
foreign ministry of the Presidency, the Secretary General of the General
Secretariat of the Council of Ministers, and the Secretary General of the
Commission. This is done in a draft form on the eve of the first day of the
European Council and submitted to the delegations early in the morning of
the next day – in time for breakfeast reading. The communique is finalised at

the end of the European Council.

23 See P.S. da C. Pereira, 'The use of a Secretariat', in Alfred Pijpers, Elfriede Regelsberger and Wolfgang Wessels, eds, European Political Cooperation in the 1980s, 1988, p. 88.

24 In this context see Vornbaumen, *Dynamik in der Swangsjacke*, p. 33.

25 Wallace and Edwards, 'European Community', p. 538.

26 For further details see note 16 in chapter 1.

27 Wallace and Edwards, 'European Community', p. 549.

28 Troy Johnston, 'The European Council', p. 23.

29 Ibid., p. 22.

30 Bonvicini and Regelsberger, 'The decision-making process', p. 161.

31 de Bassompierre, 1988, *Changing the Guard*, p. 153.

32 Different preparation periods usually prevail: 12 to 18 months for European Councils and general technical aspects in the running of the Presidency, and 6 to 10 months on policy priorities.

33 For further details on the Troika system see note 46 in this chapter.

34 For details on the transport system case see William Nicoll and Trevor C. Salmon, *Understanding the European Communities*, London, 1990, pp. 186–7.

35 Troy Johnston, 'The European Council', p. 9.

36 The Spanish government met some of these shortcomings by arranging special EC training courses for civil servants in Madrid and by sending a group of diplomats to the European Institute for Public Administration in Maastricht. Also three diplomats were asked to tour EC capitals in order to obtain additional experience.

37 Michael Garthe, 'Bundesrepublik Deutschland', in Wolfgang Wessels and Werner Weidenfeld, eds, *Jahrbuch Europaische Integration 1987/88*, Bonn, 1988, p. 348.

38 See Simon Bulmer and William Paterson, *The Federal Republic of Germany and the European Community*, London, 1988.

39 For details on the Danish Folketing see note 42 in chapter 1 of this book.

40 de Bassompierre, 1988, *Changing the Guard*.

41 Bonvicini and Regelsberger, 'The decision-making process', p. 155.

42 Robert Putnam, 'The Western economic summits: a political interpretation', in Cesare Merlini, ed., *Economic Summits and Western Decision-Making*, London, 1984, p. 213.

43 Helen Wallace, 'The Presidency of the Council of Ministers of the European Communities: a comparative perspective', in O Nuallain, ed., in collaboration with Hoscheit, *The Presidency of the European Council*, p. 276.

5

The Presidency at work

Introduction

The dictum that the Commission proposes and the Council of Ministers disposes has been widely ridiculed as being out of step with reality. Both the proposing and the disposing qualities were questioned in the 1970s and early 1980s; with the Commission being seen as a quasi-secretariat of the Council of Ministers and the latter declassed as an instrument of the European Council. By contrast, the role of the Council Presidency was viewed as both contributing to and benefiting from the influential role of the European Council.

The Single European Act of 1986 (SEA) seems to have affected the role of the Euopean Council in EC decision-making by reinstating some of the validity of the original dictum about relations between the Commission and the Council of Ministers. The SEA might also have limited the role of the Council Presidency as an initiator, power-broker and influencer of EC decision-making. The SEA has effectively advanced decision-making by reinforcing the powers of the Commission, (as well as those of the EP,) by introducing majority voting for the bulk of provisions for the completion of the internal market, and by proposing a timetable. The role of the Commission in initiation and mediation has been strengthened, the Council of Ministers is able to take decisions more rapidly and frequently and is less often forced to refer to the European Council as the final arbitrator. The manoeuvrability of the Presidency is curtailed because it needs to relate closely to the Commission's timetable or the guidelines provided for in both the Commission's 1985 White Paper, and the SEA.

The Presidency provides opportunities but these should not be equated with presidential power akin to the US system. The office bears certain privileges, like setting policy priorities, obtaining information, and determining the agenda, e.g. influencing the nature of debate and the timing of decisions for legislative adoption. It gives a government the opportunity to draw attention to themselves. Against that, the Presidency has no executive powers, e.g. vetoes or sanction possibilities. It co-ordinates proceedings within the various Council or COREPER group meetings with the intention of finding a consensus or winning formula, but it remains one of twelve equals in the EC negotiating forum.[1] Decisions have to be taken by all twelve member states and involve compromises, if not sacrifices, of national interest. The degree of manoeuvrability held by a Presidency in consensus-building is subject to considerable uncertainties emanating, for example, from the general economic and political conditions in which member states find themselves at a given time. These have included, for example, external events like the 1986 Chernobyl nuclear accident or recent events in Eastern Europe, unresolved problems or outstanding reforms of the EC,[2] and the general attitudes of governments towards integration. Such influences can add to the vagaries of competing national interests and can either harden or relax a given national negotiation position. As a consequence, gaps can appear between the policy programme put forward in the beginning and the output achieved at the end of a Presidency. Needless to say, a Presidency carries responsibility and a punishing workload which can be particularly burdensome for small countries.

Nonetheless, some Presidencies seem to do better than others under adverse conditions. For example, a comparison of Presidencies between 1986 and 1989 shows that some have been more successful than others either with regard to a range of policy objectives or in helping to solve acute problems. This raises a number of questions about the Presidency and the office holder; the extent to which the Presidency carries power irrespective of the office holder or the extent to which influence of the Presidency depends on the power position of the office holder.[3] For example, is size, experience, commitment and political clout of the office holder a decisive factor in influencing the course of events? Were the more successful Presidencies confronted with less pressing problems, more conducive circumstances (economic, political and institutional climate), or were they endowed with more organisational resources, experience and brokerage skills?

To explore these questions we need to know more about the

economic and political climate in which Presidencies operate, the
prevailing attitudes of member states towards integration and the
general level of co-operation within the EC. Next an examination of
the policy priorities is in order. How do Presidencies combine
national with Community interest?; long-term goals with six-
monthly aims?; and inherited tasks with new initiatives? What
methods do they use for achieving stipulated aims or coping with
'unexpected' events, e.g. the way the agenda is being set, and the
form in which compromise solutions are introduced? Another aspect
to examine is the way in which the Presidency seeks to promote
co-operation with the Commission and the EP. Finally, the performance of the Presidency needs to be dealt with. The slowness with
which EC problems are resolved (CAP, budget, transport, fiscal
policy, etc.) has obvious implications for what can be achieved
within six months. A distinction is thus required between actual
decisions and considerable preparatory work for decisions; between
decisions over important issues and less important ones (quality
versus quantity); and between the successful contributions of
the Presidency and those of other member states or EC institutions.
These will be examined comparatively in this chapter and used for an
evaluation of the role and importance of the Presidency.

The countries who have held the Presidency between 1986 and
1989 include 'old hands' with years of experience in EC affairs
(Belgium, France, the Netherlands, and West Germany); countries
who had the Presidency for the third time (Denmark and the United
Kingdom); Greece who had its second turn; and Spain, which after
three years of EC membership, had its first go. Four of these
countries had right-of-centre administrations (Denmark, the
Netherlands, West Germany, and the United Kingdom), and one a
left-of-centre (Spain). Changes in the political composition of
governments occurred in France, Belgium, Greece and Portugal.[4]

The findings in this chapter will be based on a series of interviews
with Foreign Office officials in eight EC member states and officials
of EC institutions.[5]

The Setting

When planning for a Presidency, among the main concerns are the
domestic, EC and international economic and political climate,
organisational resources and expertise, and ongoing EC internal and

external tasks. Of these, the surrounding economic and political climate is particularly important in that it can influence the negotiating position of individual governments and thus have bearings on the prospects for consensus or compromise. Deep-seated economic difficulties (high unemployment, high inflation and low growth rates) can either, (as was the the case in the 1970s,) result in a hardening of national positions, or encourage, (as in the beginning of the 1980s,) a Community solution. A country's basic approach must also be considered. As Helen Wallace suggests it is unrealistic to expect governments to act out of character for the six months duration of the Presidency. Rather, the framework of their general attitude to the EC and the particular interests which concern them will influence their behaviour and margin of manoeuvre.[6]

In the following a brief review of the main economic and political conditions between 1986 and 1989 will be attempted, together with a short examination of the basic dispositions of the countries which held the Presidency towards European unification. This section will be rounded off with a list of the important events, both within and outside the EC, and an exploration of the main expectations held at the start of the six monthly Presidencies.

The economic and political situation

With regard to the economic situation, there were general improve-ments in EC growth, inflation and unemployment terms over the period concerned.[7] Whereas the Community had lost 1,800,000 jobs between 1982 and 1984, it had created 3,200,000 between 1985 and 1987, and was expected to create 5 million between 1988 and 1990.[8] However, unemployment, particularly long-term unem-ployment, was still at an unacceptable high of 16.5 million in 1989. Moreover, the stock market crash of October 1987 adversely affected the economic outlook and gave rise to pessimism regarding the prospects for continued economic growth. On the other hand, the appearance of the Checcini Report in 1988 predicted substantial economic growth and lower prices for goods with the completion of the internal market by 1992.[9]

With regard to the political situation, as Figure 5.1 shows, only the British and the Greek Presidencies were free of general elections or referenda either in their own or in other member states. Spain had to cope with general elections in Ireland, Luxembourg and Greece, and direct elections to the European Parliament in all EC countries; West

	1985	1986	1987	1988	1989
Portugal	RS/6.11 –PM;FO;FI;IM;SO	PE/26.1 & 16.2	GR/3.4 · GE/19.7 EP/19.7 RS/17.8 FO: SO		
Ireland		RS/13.2 –FI;SO;EN;IM R/26.6	GR/20.1 GE/17.2 RS/10.3 –PM;FO;FI;AG;SO;IM;EN R/26.5	RS/24.11 –FI;IM	RS/10.6 –FO GE/15.6 · RS/12.7 –FO;IM
Italy	PE/3.7	GR/27.6 · RS/1.8 –FI;IM;SO;EN	GR/3.3 RS/18.4 –PM;FI;IM;SO;EN GE/14.6 · R:/8-9.11 GR/9.7 RS/29.7 –PM;FI;SO;IM;EN	GR/11.3 RS/13.4 –PM;FI;AG	GR/19.5 · RS/23.7 –PM;FO;FI;SO
Luxembourg		RS/14.7 –EM EN			
NL		GE/21.5 · RS/10.2 –IM RS/21.5 –EN			GE/RS/18.6 –FI;SO;AG;EN GR/3.5 · GE/6.9 RS/7.11 –FI;IM;SO;EN
UK	RS/2-17.9 –EN;IM		GE/RS/11.6 –AG;SO;IM		GE/24.7 –FO;IM;AG;EN RS/26-30.10 –FO;FI

Belgium	RS/7.1 –FI	GE/13.10 RD/28.11 –FI; IM			GR/19.10 GE/13.12	RS/9.5 Fi:IM.SO GR/19.10		RS/19.6 –FO
Denmark		R/27.2 RS/12.3 –AG; SO			GE/8.9 RS/10.9 –IM, AG, SO:EN	GR/14.4 GE/10.5 RS/3.6 –IM;EN		
West Germany	SE/10.3 SAARLAND WEST BERLIN SE/12.5 NORTH-RHINE WESTPHALIA	SE/15.6 LOWER SAXONY	SE/12.10 BAVARIA	GE/25.1 RS/11.3 –EN	SE/13.9 BREMEN SCHL. HOLST.	SE/20.3 BADEN-W	RS/29.11 –IM	SE/WEST BERLIN 29.1 SE/HESSE: 12.3 RS/13.4 –FI; IM PE/23.5
Greece	GE/2.6 RS/26.7 –FI; IM	RS/24.4 –IM	RS/30.10 –SO; IM	RS/5.2 –IM	RS/22.9 –SO; IM RS/26.11 –IM	RS/21.6	RS/16.11 –SO RS/15.10 –IM	RS/17.3 –EN; IM GE/18.6 / RS/2.7 –PM; –FO FI:IM. –SO:EN GE/5.11 RS/23.11 –PM; FO:FI:IM.SO:EN
Spain	RS/3.7 –FO –FI IM	R/12.3 GE/22.6 SE/22.6 ANDALUSIA	RS/26.7 –SO	SE/10.6 EP/10.6		SE/29.5 CATALUNIA	RS/8.7 –IM.SO	GE/29.10
France	GE/16.3 RS/20.3 –PM; FO: FI:IM. AG; SO:EN					PE/24.4 and 8.5 RS/12.5 –PM; FO: FI: SO:IM. AG:EN and 12.6 RS/28.6 –SO	R/6.11	

Fig. 5.1 **Elections and government changes, 1985–9**
Source: Keesing's Record of World Events, XXXI–XXXVI, 1985–90

Germany experienced general elections in Denmark and France and, presidential elections in France; Denmark was confronted with general elections in Portugal, the United Kingdom, Belgium and a referendum in Italy; the Netherlands witnessed general elections in France and Spain and a referendum in Spain. Importantly, Denmark and the Netherlands had elections in their own countries during their respective Presidencies. France was confronted with three general elections in other member states, and Belgium had the misfortune of five general elections in other member states, Spanish elections to the EP, plus a national referendum in Ireland. In other words, general elections took place in all Community countries during 1986 and 1989, with 2 such elections occurring in France, Greece, Ireland, and Spain (altogether 16 general elections). EP elections took place in all countries in 1989; a procedure Spain and Portugal had both undertaken in 1987 as well. Besides a number of state elections in West Germany there were also a substantial number of local elections; the latter have not been counted here.

If a distinction is made between the four most populous EC countries and the rest, then the French general elections during the Dutch and the West German Presidencies (plus the French presidential elections during the West German Presidency) and the British, Italian and West German elections during the Belgian Presidency weigh particularly heavily. As Leo Tindemans, the Belgian Foreign Minister, pointed out, the convergence of a number of national elections during the Belgian Presidency 'was paralysing in its effect'.[10] Coalition stress or prolonged inability to form a coalition can be an additional disruptive factor. Once again Belgium suffered from the four-month Italian coalition crisis, and Belgium itself caused disquiet during the Danish and West German Presidencies when, over a five-month period, it was unable to form a governing coalition. However, considering the stress of 'cohabitation' in the French coalition between 1986 and 1988 and the closeness to the French presidential elections, the achievement of the emergency EC summit in Brussels during the West Germany Presidency, is particularly significant. Nonetheless, as Helen Wallace points out the: 'dislocating consequences of changes of government are less problematic for those countries in which a broad consensus on EC issues persists across political parties, than for those in which distinctive party views obtain, or where attitudes towards the EC are evolving'.[11] Belgium belongs to those countries where elections seem to have less of an effect on EC policy given the virtual unanimity which prevails across party political lines on this issue.[12]

Another potential disrupting factor is the occurrence of referenda during a Presidency. Both the Danish referendum of 1986 and the Irish referendum of 1987, (during the Dutch and Belgian Presidencies respectively), related to the SEA and the future of the EC and, therefore, had direct implications on the priorities, agenda-setting and consensus-building of these Presidencies.

Orientation towards integration

There was generally a strong and stable public support in favour of European unification during the period in question, e.g. those who say that the EC is a good thing. The exception was Denmark which until the spring of 1990, was among the lowest with 44 per cent public support.[13] However, West Germany had a drop in support in 1987–88 which might have had something to do with the dispute between West Germany and the Commission over agricultural reform, steel subsidies, and beer regulations.[14] Moreover, there were relatively low turnouts in the 1989 EP direct elections (average of 57.2% for all twelve countries) with below 50 per cent ratings in Denmark, France, the Netherlands and the UK. The fact that the latter scored the lowest (41.8%) might have been influenced by Thatcher's Bruges speech in the autumn of 1988, which was highly critical of further integration.

Whether measured by public opinion, elite perception or government attitude, different commitments to the process of integration can be noted; with Belgium, France, the Netherlands, Spain and West Germany occupying one side of the spectrum, and Denmark, Greece and the United Kingdom the other. This demarcation holds, by and large, with regard to the SEA. Whereas Britain and Denmark see it mostly as the accomplishment of a free-trade area and, therefore, as an end in itself, the other countries perceive it as a stepping stone towards further economic and political unification. Whereas the Benelux countries, France, West Germany and Spain explicitly advocate such a link or toll on the virtues of political union, Britain and Denmark either consciously play down the political connotations,[15] or avoid such expressions altogether.[16] For the UK a Community of independent sovereign nations would do better than a giant new European state. Similarly, differences emerge over moves towards Economic and Monetary Union, the establishment of a

European Central Bank, the harmonisation of fiscal policy, and the abolition of border controls. Part of the reason for this might be found in differences over the insistence on national identity,[17] supposed national character or habits, e.g. British pragmatism and commonsense approach versus French Cartesian logic, strategic thinking and planning. For example, Mrs Thatcher was proud of pointing out that 'we have our eyes more on the ground rather than on the distant horizons' and 'concentrate on the down-to-earth topics leading to actions of direct and practical benefits'.[18]

However, the above demarcation into two sets of countries does not hold over the issue of enlarged powers for the European Parliament; France advocates modest increases and Greece favours more extensive EP powers.[19] Both Denmark and Britain emphasise change, not in the powers of the EP but in the relationship between the EP and the Council, e.g. more consultation.[20] In contrast Belgium, Holland, Italy, Spain and West Germany advocate more rights for the EP.

Having examined the economic, political and attitudinal aspects which affect the role of Presidencies, attention will now turn to the linkage between the tasks and expectations of Presidencies.

Chronology and expectations

After the successful introduction of the SEA, and the admittance of Portugal and Spain as EC members in 1986, the Community underwent a period of regeneration and consolidation. The Dutch Presidency in the first half of 1986 had to complete the signing of the SEA, which in the Danish case required a national referendum. The signed, but not yet ratified, SEA underwent an experimental application during the Dutch, British and Belgian Presidencies (January 1986 to June 1987). For the Dutch, the entry of Portugal and Spain required additional adjustment. In view of these circumstances, the Dutch were careful 'not to pitch hopes too high'[21] and to put the emphasis on the implementation of the internal market. Britain took a similar stance. An additional problem which befell the British Presidency was how to cope with the post-Chernobyl situation and the growing problem of CAP and financial reforms. According to Geoffrey Howe, Britain took over the Presidency 'with a mixture of trepidation, hope and determination'.[22]

The problem of CAP and financial reform, conveniently postponed at the 1986 London European Council, loomed large at the beginning of the Belgian Presidency in 1987. Indeed Delors was asked to undertake a tour of Capitals by the London European Council of December 1986. The tentative conclusions reached at the Reagan–Gorbachev Reykjavik summit in October 1986, on the abolition of nuclear missiles, had also ruffled the feathers of European leaders. The summit demonstrated the lack of consultation with the Europeans by the Americans and seemingly exposed the vulnerability of the Europeans in security terms. In addition, Belgium anticipated a number of elections in other member states. Subsequently, Leo Tindemans, the Belgian foreign minister, saw few possibilities in January 1987 of promoting the process of integration. He even went as far as to suggest that 'considering what Belgium was confronted with one could be inclined to be distraught and dispense with the Presidency'.[23] The, unsurprising, failure of the Brussels European Council of June 1987 to make an effective impact on the Delors package[24] meant that problems and pressures were mounting by the time Denmark was starting its turn in the Presidency in the second half of 1987. With the positive outcome of the Irish referendum in May 1987, the SEA was formally ratified and its decision-making reforms (co-operation and assent procedures and majority voting) could officially be applied from 1 July 1987. Under this dual challenge of the pending Delors' package and the formal start of the SEA, Ellemann-Jensen, the Danish foreign minister, 'sought to be realistic in the presentation of Danish priorities' and to avoid 'any great initiative on what we want'.[25] Though progress was made during the Danish Presidency on the adoption of the Delors reforms, major disagreements over agricultural reforms between Britain and West Germany continued. Consequently, the Copenhagen European Council of December 1987 ended in failure and without a communique.

Being partly responsible for the continuing legacy of the Delors package, the West German Presidency made major efforts at the beginning of 1988 to find a solution which came via the Brussels emergency European Council in February 1988. The West Germany Presidency followed this success with an impressive number of provisions being adopted from the Commission's White Paper, initiatives in EC external matters, and the launch of a study on how to establish EMU. The newly found dynamism, if not euphopria, instilled self-confidence in subsequent Presidencies[26] and encouraged attempts to link the internal market programme with monetary, social and environmental objectives of the SEA in particular. Moreover, East-West confrontation began to thaw significantly, a factor the Greek Presidency seized upon and sought to promote further. By the time the Spanish Presidency began its term, in the first half of 1989, the difficult issues of the internal market programme (such as fiscal policy, company law, merger controls, etc.) began to surface more cogently, and the Delors Committee[27] was expected to present its report on EMU. Therefore a mixture of expectations and concerns prevailed. The latter were coloured by the fact that Spain was a complete novice in the experience of EC presidencies. In addition, it was faced with a new Commission and the prospect of direct elections to the EP in June 1989. Foreign Minister Fernandez-Ordonez reflected on this when he stressed that the Spanish programme was 'modest and realistic in its expectations'.[28] Spain did better than generally expected, especially with regard to internal market matters and monetary co-operation. Hopes were high when France took over the Presidency in the second half of 1989, the year of its bicentenary celebrations, and a newly elected EP, expectations were high. It was hoped that France, which had traditionally tried for the spectacular, would become the torchbearer for the adoption of the European Social Charter, which had been narrowly missed at the Madrid European Council of June 1989, and become the trail-blazer for an Intergovernmental Conference on EMU. Equally, great strides were expected in the internal market programme. However, Roland Dumas, the French Foreign Minister, was careful not to let such great expectations colour the course of events and stressed instead that France was 'not too ambitious in its objectives'.[29]

The priorities

As the outline above suggests, the selection of policy priorities of Presidencies is influenced by general economic and political conditions, by countries' basic dispositions regarding European unification, and, most importantly, by the general Community time-table.[30] In turn, this timetable reflects either recurring issues, like the annual budgetary and agricultural price review, or pre-arranged Community commitments and objectives, like the SEA programme, renewal of external trade or aid and co-operation agreements, anniversary celebrations[31] and 'year themes'.[32] In addition to the Commission's timetable, there are EPC mandates. Presidencies are, therefore, not enclosed epochs but merely phases of an ongoing process.[33] This was recognised in the decision by the Luxembourg, Dutch and British Presidencies to initiate a 'rolling' Presidency on internal market matters in 1985–6 i.e. not to attempt to achieve everything in one Presidency but over successive ones.

The empirical evidence suggests that in general terms, the Presidencies under review let the Commission set the agenda for the major issues, such as the internal market, the Delors package, and EMU, in a way not witnessed prior to 1986.[34] However, the French Presidency of 1989 reinstated a more independent line, especially in a response to events in Eastern Europe. In the following, the Presidencies' priorities will be briefly examined with regard to the internal market programme, the other SEA objectives, and EC external policies.

Internal market
All eight presidencies referred to the completion of the internal market as a major priority. They followed consistently the Commission's timetable and guidelines, but inserted their own specific interests where possible. Examples of the latter included the Dutch emphasis on transport policy, especially road haulage (a traditional Dutch interest); the British stress on financial services, in line with the introduction of the 'big bang' in 1986 and its competitive edge in the financial sector. The accent on air transport fares and public procurement can also be related to British market advantages and privatisation interests. Denmark's high standards in environmental policy and consumer protection, were reflected in demands for action in these fields e.g. the curbing of emission from motor vehicles and the improvement and harmonisation of food law. West Germany insisted more explicitly on progress in company law, because of the potential migration of German firms to other EC countries which do not have similar company structures or worker participation arrangements. Given their large farming population, it is not surprising that both Greece and Spain highlighted their concern over harmonisation measures on agricultural machinery and veterinary issues. In line with its national emphasis on research and development (witness the French initiative on Eureka), France laid particular stress on progress in the telecommunications and audio-visual sectors.[35]

Other SEA objectives

Whilst the SEA laid out a number of objectives, it made no provisions for financial arrangements. Any attempt to do so faced a multitude of related items, chief among which were agricultural reforms as well as British budgetary rebates.[36] In February 1987, Delors boldly introduced a proposal in which he combined the issue of agricultural and financial reforms with the question of regional aid. The Belgian, Danish, West German and Greek[37] Presidencies were confronted with the adoption and implementation of this package. By the time the Spanish took over the Presidency the three-fold concern of the Delors package had become a minor concern, but the monetary issue had come prominently to the fore.

Three factors may explain why it took until 1988 before monetary co-operation became a specific concern in the priorities of Council Presidencies: the absorption of the Community in the solution of the Delors package in 1987, the stock-market crash of October 1987; and increasing Franco–German co-operation.[38] West Germany thus became the first Presidency to strive for the EMU, call for a strengthening of the EMS, and the establishment of a European Central Bank. As a consequence, a decision was taken at the Hannover European Council in June 1988 to establish a committee aimed at exploring how and when EMU could be phased in. This committee, consisting primarily of governors of national central banks, was headed by Jacques Delors and is subsequently known as the 'Delors Committee'. The Spanish Presidency prepared for dealing with the findings of the Delors committee and sought to 'make as much progress as possible in defining the necessary stages for achieving monetary union'.[39] Similarly, after the positive decision at the Madrid European Council in June 1989, the French Presidency declared that it wanted 'to organise its work so that the European Council in Strasbourg can express an opinion on the progress achieved over the whole area of EMU'.[40]

The idea that the single market must be linked with economic growth, higher standards of living, a better quality of life together with progress in the social field, grew slowly on EC member states. There was, and still is, dispute over whether social Europe is an integral part of economic Europe or whether it is a by-product of it.[41] Subsequently, whilst the Commission consistently proposed measures to improve the employment situation, promote vocational training, and raise health and safety standards in the workplace, measures backed by successive Presidencies, it was only during the Greek Presidency that the Commission came up with its blueprint for a European Charter for Basic Social Rights.[42] Though Greece had declared the social dimension a priority, the delay by the Commission in presenting specific proposals gave the Spanish and French Presidencies the opportunity to take up this task with more vigour. Like Greece, both had socialist administrations and were thus particularly keen to see the social dimension developed.

The Chernobyl effect, the Seveso incident,[43] the spread of acid rain, and the 'greenhouse' factor became the basis for the Commission's proposals of 1987 regarding air and water pollution, disposal of dangerous waste, and the ozone layer. In turn, these became concerns of the Presidencies, especially those of Denmark, West Germany and Greece, the latter expressing particular concern over pollution in the Mediterranean Sea. However, on the whole, these Commission efforts were reactive and haphazard attempts rather than systematic efforts to construct an environmental policy. The Commission's own omission was recognised by Delors when he remarked that the issue of the environment had been approached with greater dynamism by the Hannover European Council than by the Commission.[44]

The SEA, in Article 130 I, stipulates the adoption by the Community of multi-annual research and development framework programmes. Efforts to do so occurred during the Dutch, British, Belgian and Danish Presidencies. It fell on successive Presidencies to emphasise specific programmes, like ESPRIT, BRITE, RACE, etc.

External relations
External relations consist of trade, aid and development, and EPC matters. External trade issues were a recurrent theme during all eight Presidencies, involving, for example, GATT (either via the Uruguay Round, or the Multifibre Agreement),[45] the USA, Japan, ASEAN, EFTA and COMECON countries.

Renewal of the Lome Convention came up during the 1987 Belgian Presidency and continued until it was concluded during the French Presidency in 1989. The Belgian Presidency had also proposed a compensation system for the least developed countries' export revenues, and the Spanish Presidency advocated steps to overcome the debt problem of middle-income countries (especially in Latin America) through the establishment of a European

Guarantee Fund.

Unlike EC external trade, or aid and co-operation policy, EPC is an intergovernmental exercise. On EPC the Presidency is supposed to initiate proposals, implement the decisions and discuss them with third countries. EPC tasks often involve mandates for either the Presidency or the Troika,[46] and entail 'missions' to third countries. As pointed out by Helen Wallace, 'EPC make ministerial interventions both more influential and less predictable than in Community business, where the options are more circumscribed, the room for manoeuvre is generally limited and the weight of precedent and existing commitments is often overbearing'.[47] EPC is heavily influenced by external events such as the CSCE dialogue, UN proceedings, regional conflicts (Middle East, Central America, South Africa, Afghanistan, South East Asia) and arms control agreements between the USA and the Soviet Union. Though EPC is mostly reactive, there were also a number of Presidency initiatives. For example, Britain emphasised issues of international drug trafficking and international terrorism; Denmark initiated the first EC–USA foreign ministers meeting; West Germany tried to make progress on common guidelines for arms exports; Greece tried to initiate a political dialogue with Eastern European countries. Spain, initiated contacts with all the participants in the Middle East conflict,[48] and relaunched the Euro–Arab Dialogue; while France advanced the idea of establishing a European Bank for Reconstruction and Development. Both the German and the French initiatives are also examples of a tendency by Presidencies to combine EPC and external trade matters.

The methods

Presidencies cannot switch programmes, but they can select certain priorities within a given parameter, or provide political impetus. Going a step further, even though a Presidency is confronted with ongoing Community work programmes, this work needs to be shaped and decisions have to be taken about whether a given issue is 'ripe' for COREPER or Council meetings. As van den Broek, the Dutch Foreign Minister, points out 'an active Presidency is not simply tolerated, it is required and expected'.[49] What then distinguishes an active from a passive Presidency? How does an active Presidency live up to its role as a stimulant, interlocuteur and broker?

For analytical reasons three interrelated styles can be identified: style of engagement, style of agenda-setting, and style of arbitration.

Style of engagement
The way Presidencies engage themselves relates to their basic orientation towards integration and to the way they interpret their role under certain climates or conditions. For example, the Dutch regarded their Presidency primarily as 'a service to the Community and political co-operation'. Their aims were to concentrate on the 'management and technical part' of Community business. Greece saw its role largely as an administrator and expediter and put the emphasis on practical decisions. The UK Presidency tried to portray itself as a 'normal and engaged member', to repeat its previous record of 'solid management', and to strive for a 'harmonious' European Council – one reason, perhaps, why the UK refused to deal with the looming financial and agricultural crisis.[50] Whereas West Germany put the emphasis on 'responsibility', Spain highlighted the 'dignity' of running the Presidency.

Presidencies attempt to communicate their aims and to canvass the views of other governments and EC institutions on these aims.[51] They make use of a variety of communication methods. In most cases the incumbent president (a head of state or government) sends letters to his/her counterparts inviting them to take additional steps on, for example, the adoption of provisions of the Commission's 1985 White Paper. Presidents also undertake visits to other countries for the same or similar Community purposes; sometimes, as in the Belgian case, a tour of all capitals takes place before a pending European Council meeting. Equally, bilateral talks, which may over-lap with the routine meetings among governments, are arranged involving Ministers and civil servants. Of considerable importance is Franco–German co-operation which often results in joint EC initiatives or compromises. One attempt at such a compromise occurred at the Brussels emergency Summit in February 1988 which helped to lay the groundwork for agricultural reforms, especially on Monetary Compensatory Amounts (MCAs) and cereal thresholds. The establishment of so-called 'national co-ordinators', on, for example, the free movement of people, has been yet another instru-ment for the Presidency to carry out its tasks more effectively.[52] However, a main characteristic of style of engagement relates to the extent to which Presidencies pursue an innovative role rather than the role of a manager. The extent to which the Presidency engages in routine tasks, deals with the 'rolling' agenda of the internal market troika or carries out prevailing EPC mandates should be distinguished from a Presidency which acts as an innovator. West Germany, on EMU, and France, in dealing with regime changes in Eastern Europe, were two Presidencies which used their role in an innovative way.

Style of agenda-setting

Besides having to decide when, a Presidency also has to determine how, to put an item on the agenda. A Presidency might have made clear the objectives, and might have got backing for them from the Commission, but it makes quite a difference how this priority is put on the agenda. A Presidency has, first of all, a choice over the type of Council of Ministers' meeting it wants to arrange, e.g. a formal or an informal one. Secondly, it must determine whether to put up an item for a decision or for a point of debate. Thirdly, it has flexibility over whether to call for an 'A' or 'B' point procedure.[53]

It has become customary to call for informal Council meetings at the beginning of the Presidency's term. Although usually no decision-making takes place in informal meetings,[54] they offer the chance to explain informally the intentions of the Presidency and to explore the possibilities for decision-making by the formal Councils. The Greek suggestion to hold an informal meeting of the Social Council serves as an interesting illustration of the question of choice. On the one hand, it had declared social policy a top priority, and had sent a memo to this effect to the Commission three months prior to the beginning of its Presidency. Therefore one or two formal Council of Ministers' meetings dealing with social policy would have seemed to be appropriate. On the other hand, Greece had no concrete points on which to proceed formally since the Commission had been unable, until November 1988, to finalise the content of its own proposals. This highlights the importance of the Commission and demonstrates that what is desirable from the Presidency's point of view is not always possible from the Commission's perspective. It was sensible for the Danish Presidency to make the first Internal Market Council meeting an informal one in order to acquaint ministers with the new rules. This is particularly true given the amount of preparatory work done by the Belgian, British and Dutch Presidencies in 1986–7 and the fact that the SEA became fully operative in July 1987. It is interesting to note that both an emergency and an extraordinary European Council were held during the West German and French Presidencies respectively. After the Reykjavik debacle of October 1986 Delors made a similar request to the British Presidency, but was turned down.

Style of arbitration

As a general rule, it is easier to find agreement on questions that unite than it is to resolve those that divide or threaten to divide. On the other hand, what is needed are texts which are acceptable, not those with which everyone necessarily agrees, e.g. it is not necessary to win over every delegation but to produce a text which every delegation can live with, or which is sufficiently close for a delegation not to obstruct.

On most internal market issues a Presidency has to decide when to call for a vote and when to continue to seek agreement. The acceptance of majority voting as the general practice makes members of the Council more eager to accept compromises before a vote takes place. Greece speeded up the process of majority voting; Spain and France followed. However, formal votes are not always taken in cases where the Presidency feels that the necessary majority prevails.[55] Sometimes, however, a country purposely wants to be outvoted in order to demonstrate to a domestic audience its inability to secure the outcome it wanted.[56] Generally, the aim within the Council of Minister is to seek consensus, and there has, as yet, been no insistence on the veto with regard to internal market issues.[57]

Against the role model which depicts the Presidency as an arbitrator, a Presidency also seeks to defend its own interests. There are limits, however, on the extent to which the latter can be done. A Presidency must avoid being seen to abuse power, as trust is lost between the participants. On the other hand, it also must also be seen to avoid deadlock, splits or isolation of a country or group of countries at either the level of the Council of Ministers or European Council. In short, it must place the emphasis on the exercise of 'good office'. Belgium, in its 1987 Presidency tried to keep the Delors package together but faced great difficulties. These difficulties resulted from a number of diverse but interrelated sources. They included Italian and Portuguese objections to financial reform, British demands for an EC budgetary discipline and rebate, and West German and British differences over the reduction of CAP expenditures and the phasing-in of cereal quotas. French and German disputes over the maintenance of MCAs, and Danish and Dutch objections to large-scale CAP reforms were other points of disagreement. Finally, the Mediterranean countries and Ireland, were at odds with Britain and Germany over the increase of structural funds for the poorer regions. Under these circumstances, although Belgium had the Delors package discussed by the Permanent Representative Committee every week and considered by the General Affairs Council in April, May and June of 1987, it could not have it carried at the European Council in Brussels in June 1987. As Prime Minister Martens remarked: 'At a given moment [during the Presidency] it would undoubtedly have been possible to achieve unanimity, but that would have resulted in conclusions drawn in Brussels being much less clear and in fact meaningless'.[58] The Belgian insistence on the total package thus avoided a provisional or short-term solution which would have undermined attempts to seek long-term progress on agricultural, financial and regional aid questions. Even worse, according to Wilfred Martens: 'any attempt to rush . . . would have doomed the European Council meeting to failure and created divisions within the Community which would have taken a long time to heal'.[59]

The Danish Presidency of 1987 continued in the effort to avoid splits and the isolation of one or a group of countries. To achieve this it decided to prepare the Copenhagen European Council of December 1987 in a different way by sending a set of draft conclusions (drawn up by the Presidency) before the meeting, (a substantial document of 35 to 40 pages) to give colleagues an opportunity to have a thorough discussion with their governments at home on the total solution. The Danes assumed, with some justification, that the Presidency's memorandum would be the only possible basis for a compromise.[60] However, the other delegations maintained their positions. This was most noticeable in the opposing views of Britain and West Germany. On the other hand, by refusing to apply COREPER to the British budgetary problem, the Danish Presidency showed inflexibility towards a solution of the Delors' package at COREPER level which might have helped to prepare matters for the Copenhagen Summit. The Danish view was that this matter could only be dealt with at higher level.[61]

Chancellor Kohl, during the West Germany Presidency of the first half of 1988, also sent a suggested compromise to other EC leaders[62] which, unlike the ill-fated Danish one, produced results. According to Genscher this was 'because each of us was ready to compromise, everyone benefited'.[63] Though it is debatable whether British gains were commensurate with their initial demands for agricultural and financial reform, it was an acceptable compromise. That such outcomes are the exception rather than the rule became evident in the Spanish Presidency at the Madrid European Council in June 1989 when it tried to promote the adoption of the European Social Charter and the Delors Committee Report on EMU. Once again the Presidency's handling avoided greater damage through the postponement of the Social Charter adoption, and a compromise formula over the adoption of the Delors Committee recommendations.[64] As Solbes Mira pointed out, 'the Madrid Summit avoided a breach which was not a situation of 10 to 2 or 11 to 1, but something much deeper which would have created difficulties for integration and the building of Europe'.[65]

What then are the factors which determine an active or strong presidency? Are the willingness for self sacrifice, effective leadership and sound co-operation with the Commission and the EP the key ingredients to success? There was general agreement that West Germany made a number of sacrifices.[66] These involved insurance, transport and agriculture and demonstrated courage in the face of prevailing domestic opposition, especially from farmers, and in the pending state elections. Similarly, sacrifices were made by France on road haulage, further deregulation of air travel, and on the partial opening of the telecommunications market to free competition, ending the stranglehold of the Post Telegraph and Telephones on services such as telebanking, cashpoints, and data information services. France was also willing to remove its remaining foreign-exchange controls six months earlier than the agreed deadline. In contrast, the British Presidency was accused of dragging its feet on matters relating to the pollution of the North Sea, on the control of air pollution, and on sanctions against South Africa. Though Denmark was prepared to forego national interests, especially in the agricultural sector, and to act as an honest broker, it did not get the compromise solution. Part of the reason for this might have been that it lacked political clout.

Political clout and leadership qualities

It is often maintained that small countries are the ideal brokers, particularly in situations were two or more large countries are at loggerheads. This did not hold during either the Belgian or Danish Presidency. As a matter of fact Martens, the Belgian Prime Minister, accused West Germany and Britain of systematically pursuing their own interests at the expense of the smaller countries and at the expense of progress on EC integration.[67] Rather, as the case over the adoption of the Delors package in February 1988 showed, success in EC negotiation and integration depends heavily on the political will of the larger member states. It seems that large countries, probably because of their economic and political weight, have more influence in forcing compromises than the smaller ones.[68] This is particularly so when it is combined with leadership qualities.

Leadership qualities are a necessary ingredient for an effective Presidency and need to be evident at various levels: European Council, Council of Ministers, COREPER and Working Groups. Both Helmut Kohl and Hans Dietrich Genscher were seen as providing 'strong' leadership during the West German Presidency. Such 'strength' was missing in Poul Schluter's case[69] with regard to the Danish Presidency and, due to his illness, in Papandreou's case with regard to the Greek Presidency. On the other hand, some of the individual Greek chairmen of the Council of Ministers, like Theodoros Pangalos (Alternate Minister of Foreign Affairs responsible for European Community Affairs), Panayotis Roumeliotis (National Economy), and Mrs Vasso Papandreou (Internal Market), received favourable appraisal.[70] Chairmanship of the Internal Market Council, often held by the so-called Euro-Minister, is becoming increasingly important. Leadership qualities require a great deal of understanding of the partner's positions, tact in the handling of conflictual issues, and, as far as possible, a minimum of personal likes and dislikes. The apparent difficulties between Margaret Thatcher and Helmut Kohl, and the seemingly friendly relationship between Hans Dietrich Genscher and Roland Dumas demonstrate, however, that requirements and practice do not always coincide.

Leadership qualities are also a factor in the relationship between the Presidency and the Commission as well as the EP. As Bassompiere suggests, the best results have been achieved by good teamwork between the Presidency and the Commission.[71] These results however, are not always achieved, as the relationship between Margaret Thatcher and Jacques Delors showed, not only during the British Presidency of 1986 but also subsequently. Initially, there was also a frosty relationship between the 1988 German Presidency and the Commission, because of disputes over beer regulations, steel subsidies and cereal thresholds. This improved after the joint meeting in December 1987 between the German Government and the Commission college. The French Presidency of 1989 benefited from the fact that Jacques Delors was an ex-Government colleague which helped to foster close contacts with Roland Dumas (Foreign Minister), Mrs Edith Cresson (Minister for European Affairs), and President Francois Mitterrand.

Generally there is close collaboration between the Presidency and the Commission, especially between the president of the Commission and the Foreign Minister of the country holding the Presidency.[72] This contact helps, among other things, in the formulation and finalisation of compromises. Jacques Delors has also frequently acted as a trouble-shooter and has undertaken tours of capitals, as in 1987. The Commission, whilst interested in Community progress, also shares responsibility when things go badly within the EC.[73]

Presidencies devote considerable time to maintaining a dialogue with the EP. Foreign Ministers attend the EP plenary sessions at least twice (presenting the programme and reporting on what was achieved), and there have been additional visits, especially when more than one European Council was held.[74] It has become customary for the leaders of government or heads of state to report to the EP on European Council meetings. Euro-Ministers are the most frequent visitors and they usually deal with internal market and general affairs issues. Ministers also meet EP committees. frequently; on average approximately twenty such meetings took place during each of the eight Presidencies. The Political Affairs Committee, the Agricultural, the Internal Market Committees, the Committee on Environment and Consumer Protection, the Economic and Monetary Affairs Committee and the Budget Commitee are the most visited. The Dutch even invited all the rapporteurs of EP Committees dealing with internal market matters to meetings of the Council of Ministers. However, only a few of these rapporteurs attended.[75] These contacts help to facilitate the take-up of parliamentary amendments to legislative proposals still being considered by the Council of

Ministers. It is customary for Presidencies to liaise with MEPs from their own countries in particular, e.g. to transmit information about the Presidencies' aims and actions. Chairmen of EP political groups are also regularly informed.

A Presidency is required to answer a series of written and oral questions. There is a feeling, however, that many of the oral questions posed are esoteric and can only be dealt with in a very general way. Some Presidencies even expressed disillusionment and felt they were wasting their time dealing with an 'irresponsible' and undisciplined institution.[76]

Evaluation: opportunities and constraints

Is the Presidency more of a constraint than an opportunity? The West German Presidency of 1988 demonstrated that it can be an opportunity to make a significant political impact either on national objectives or agreements on Community policies. However, more often than not the opposite can happen and constraints outweigh opportunities, e.g. burdensome routine tasks which give very little influence to the incumbent.[77] Generally speaking, there are limited opportunities for Presidencies to determine the agenda of the Community, to influence the outcome of Community policies,[78] or, for that matter, to pursue objectives of national interest. There are a number of constraints. Firstly, a Presidency is conditioned by the setting (economic, political, and institutional). Secondly, the EC is like a convoy – it moves slowly. Thirdly, the Community is not a 'Selbstzweck' but consists of a number of competing national interests and represents a forum for negotiation. The emphasis is on economic calculations about gains and losses rather than on problem-solving. Fourthly, the Presidency has no veto or sanction capability.

Though these constraints are considerable, it would be wrong to equate the influence of the Presidency with the exercise of either 'negative power' (to keep off or delay items on the agenda) or 'chance' (to claim credit for an agreement that was already on the books).[79] For one thing, the SEA has provided guidelines which Presidencies can follow; unlike the 1970s or early 1980s when Presidencies were primarily engaged in crisis-management. Secondly, the Troika principle or 'rolling' presidencies has made them more effective. Thirdly, the game involved in achieving the adoption of the 275 provisions of the Commission's White Paper, stimulates a Presidency to achieve credible results. This often motivates Presidencies to make self-sacrifices (or to forego national interests), to lend their weight to compromise solutions, and to seek extensive cooperation with the Commission and the EP.

What powers are vested in the Presidency and how important is the office holder? Though the principle of rotation gives each country, whether small or large, equal opportunities, different office holders exercise different styles of engagement, agenda setting and arbitration. Equally, they offer different leadership abilities which influence the effectiveness of the Presidency as an instrument of EC decision-making. However, the separation between the 'chair' and the office holder in terms of effectiveness cannot always be made in practice. Furthermore, whilst it can be argued that 'small countries' can (and wish to) derive more overt benefit from the extra authority of the 'chair', this factor was not found to be important in this study.

Given that Community progress comes from slow co-operation, one should avoid judging a particular Presidency by its ability either to score high on what has become the European league table of White Paper adoptions, or by its ability to achieve spectacular results. The danger with 'high scores' is that it does not differentiate quantity from quality; e.g. some pieces of legislation are of very limited importance and do not carry much weight in assessing economic advantages for member states. Yet they score just the same as other legislation which may be of greater importance for the conclusion of the internal market. The importance of preparatory work to the collective effort also deserves consideration. For example, the 1987 Danish Presidency had prepared the groundwork for a solution to the Delors package, yet it was the succeeding West German Presidency which was credited with the success. As the Danish Prime Minister Schluter complained, member states were not disposed towards a compromise at the Copenhagen Summit, even though 'they were only trifles apart'.[80]

The apex for every Presidency is the European Council. It is usually held at the end of the Presidency's term of office but can occur twice as was the case during the West German and French Presidencies and during the Irish and Italian Presidencies (all between 1988 and 1990). European Councils are a media stunt, in that they are a forum where either difficult problems are being resolved or important impulses are given for further Community development.

Wilfred Martens and Helmut Kohl, for different reasons, were credited with having restored the European Council to the role of a political instigator during their respective Presidencies. It had assumed the role of an appeal body in the late 1970s and early 1980s in the face of the impotence of the Council of Ministers and COREPER. Martens preserved and promoted the Delors package and Kohl effectively prepared the Hannover European Council of June 1988. In contrast, the unsuccessful Copenhagen Summit of December 1987 was marred by innumerable matters of detail which should have been dealt with by the portfolio ministers before going to the European Council.[81] The absence of such details enabled the European Councils of The Hague (1986) and of Hannover (1988) in particular to devote itself to its original task e.g., to the conduct of policy discussions, to develop guidelines for the future, and to discuss major international problems.[82]

Conclusion

Although, the increase of majority voting by the SEA has affected the role of the Council Presidency as an initiator, power broker and influencer, in general terms, the SEA has furthered both the management and innovative role of the Council Presidency. With the increasing volume of work brought about via the implementation of the internal market programme, more management activities were assumed by the Presidency. Similarly, the general aims raised in the SEA about social, monetary and foreign policy co-operation enabled certain Presidencies to employ an innovative role. Of the eight Presidencies examined, most sought to expand implementation of the SEA; Britain and Denmark were the exceptions. Also, most appeared prepared, to a considerable extent, to put the Community interest above the national interest. The European Council still represents the big occasion for the Council Presidency to present their six-monthly stint in a positive light. The European Council meetings during the West German, Spanish and French Presidencies (1988–9) stand out particularly well in this respect (as do those during the Irish and Italian Presidencies in 1990). They represent the main vehicle for launching new initiatives and for furthering EC integration.

Since the SEA there has been a significant improvement both in the working relationship and in the collaboration between the Council Presidency and the Commission. Old Commission ideas for downgrading the Presidency and the tendency to regard the Presidency as a dangerous rival of the Commission has all but disappeared. The emphasis is now on legislative and political planning, involving the Commission, a seamless flow of Presidencies and, increasingly, the European Parliament as well.[83] Also EC and EPC matters are coming closer together because of the increasingly political use made (by the Commission among others) of the Community's economic instruments; witness their use in 1990–1 over Eastern Europe for instance. In short, both the Presidency and the Commission engage in joint tasks and in the co-ordination of their policy objectives. The so-called Delors package of 1987 and the Delors Report on EMU of 1989 are two of the clearest expressions of joint collaboration.

Caution is, therefore, in order to neither overplay nor under-estimate the impact of the Council Presidency in EC decision-making. The Presidency provides opportunities in the setting of political priorities and in determining the agenda, but entails limitations to what can be achieved.[84] These drawbacks result from the short duration of Presidencies, the 'rolling Presidency programmes', the overlap in functions between the Presidency and the Commission, and the prevailing economic and political conditions both domestically and in other EC countries. In the final analysis, the Council Presidency deals with twelve sovereign states and their competing interests, an independent-minded Commission and an aspirational EP. It needs considerable brokerage skill, to produce a winning coalition even in situations of majority voting. These skills require, among other things, leadership qualities, political clout, the formulation of compromises or 'package' solutions, concession on its own national interest, and an effective and co-operative working relationship with the Commission and the EP. Among the eight Presidencies examined for the period 1986 to 1989, the French and West German and to some extent Spanish Presidencies combined these requirements most effectively. These Presidencies also pursued, what Helen Wallace describes as, a distinctive political objective and therefore tended to view the Presidency strategically.[85] There is no evidence, as was found in the mid 1980s,[86] that the Council Presidency has reached a plateau in the Community framework. On the contrary the indication is that the SEA has given the Council Presidency additional opportunities to play a greater and more effective role in EC decision-making.

However, whilst the overall impact of the Council Presidency on

EC decision-making cannot easily be assessed, a distinction should be made between the management and mediating performance of the Council Presidency in legislative terms on the one hand, and its performance as an innovator for new policies on the other. The dynamics of the SEA, regime changes in Eastern Europe and the Gulf conflict have acted as a stimulant for innovative measures on the part of the Presidencies between 1990 and 1991. These initiatives were mostly directed towards the Intergovernmental Conferences on EMU and Political Union. The agenda of these two conferences and the Council Presidency's role in it will be examined in the next chapter.

Notes

1   Helen Wallace, 'The Presidency of the Council of Ministers of the European Communities: a comparative perspective', in Colm O Nuallain, ed., in collaboration with Jean-Marc Hoscheit, *The Presidency of the European Council of Ministers. Impacts and Implications for National Governments*, London, 1985, p. 262.

2   For example, Leo Tindemans, the Belgian Foreign Minister, cited the delay to entry into force of the SEA as having 'disrupted the scheduling of legislative activity'. See the *Official Journal of the EC*, 16 June 1987, Office for Official Publications, Luxembourg, p. 49.

3   For a thorough analysis of this point see Axel Vornbaeumen, *Dynamik in der Zwangsjacke: Die Praesidentschaft im Ministerrat der Europaeischen Gemeinschaft als Fuehrungsinstrument*, Europa Union Verlag, Bonn, 1985.

4   These involved the period of 'cohabitation' (between socialist and right of centre parties in France) during 1986 and 1988; the formation of a grand coalition in Belgium after the December 1987 general elections; the coming to power of the Portuguese Social Democrats in 1987; and the displacement of PASOK in Greece in 1989 by a coalition between New Democracy and the Communist Party.

5   For details on officials interviewed see note 8 of chapter 1.

6   See H. Wallace, 'The Presidency of the Council of Ministers', pp. 272–3.

7   Growth, Inflation and Unemployment Rates (in percentages) between 1985 and 1989:

	1985	1986	1987	1988	1989
Growth rate	0.9	1.9	2.3	2.8	2.9
Inflation rate	5.2	2.8	3.4	4.3	5.4
Unemployment rate	10.9	10.8	10.5	10.0	9.0

Source: *Eurostatistics: Data for Short Term Analysis*, Annual Reports 1986, pp. 87–90.

8   Figures mentioned by Jacques Delors in a statement before the EP. See the *Official Journal of the EC*, Debates of the European Parliament, 26 July 1989, Office for Official Publications, Luxembourg, p. 27.

9   Paolo Cecchini with Michel Catinat and Alexis Jacquemin, *The European Challenge 1992: The Benefits of a Single Market*, (English edition by John Robinson), Aldershot, 1988.

10   Leo Tindemans, in a speech before the European Parliament, quoted in the *Official Journal of the EC*, Debates of the EP, 16 June 1987, Office for Official Publications, Luxembourg, p. 49.

11   H. Wallace, 'The Presidency of the Council of Ministers', p. 274.

12   I am indebted to John Fitzmaurice for having brought this point to my attention.

13   See Euro Barometer: Early Release, 33, 17 May 1990, p. 2.

14   For details see Elisabeth Noelle-Neumann and Gerhard Herdegen, 'Die Oeffentliche Meinung', Werner Weidenfeld and Wolfgang Wessels, eds, *Jahrbuch Europaeische Integration, 1987/88*, Bonn, 1988, pp. 316–29.

15   Witness the initial stress by British governments on the EEC rather than the EC, and the stress in late 1990 on the ERM rather than the EMS.

16   For example, the MEP Marco Pannella criticised Ellemann-Jensen, the Danish Foreign Minister for not having mentioned the words 'Political Union' once in his speech before the European Parliament in July 1987 when introducing the Danish Presidency programme. Quoted in the *Official Journal of the EC*, Debates of the EP, 8.7. 1987, Office for Official Publications, Luxembourg, p. 138.

17   For example, British reluctance to countenance the further surrender of national sovereignty to the EC reflects the instinct of a nation which has enjoyed centuries of freedom from foreign interference.

18   Quoted in the *Official Journal of the EC*, Debates of the EP., 9 December 1986, Office for Official Publications, Luxembourg, p. 43.

19   As the Greek Foreign Affairs Minister Karolos Papoulias pointed out: 'we have consistently advocated a substantial strength of the powers of the EP', quoted in the *Official Journal of the EC*, Debates of the EP, 5 February 1988, Office for Official Publications, Luxembourg, p. 31.

20   However, since the 1986 referendum, Denmark seems to have developed a somewhat more positive attitude towards the EP. Nonetheless, whilst there was more concern over the democratic deficit in 1989–90, the Danes were careful to ensure that the granting of more powers to the EP was not given at the expense of the powers of national parliaments.

21   Statement by Van den Broek, Dutch Foreign Minister, before the EP, *Official Journal of the EC*, Debates of the EP, 1 June 1986, Office for Official Publications, Luxembourg.

22   Quoted in Commission of the European Communities, *Bulletin of the EC*, 7/8, 1986, Office for Official Publications, Luxembourg, p. 144.

23   See Wichard Woyke, 'Belgien, Niederlande, Luxemburg', Weidenfeld und Wessels, eds, *Jahrbuch der Eurpaeischen Integration 1987/88*, p. 334.

24   The Delors package, submitted in February 1987, comprised agricultural and financial reforms and regional aid.

25   Quoted in the *Official Journal of the EC*, Debates of the EP, 8 July 1987, Office for Official Publications, Luxembourg, p. 142.

26   Fernandez-Ordonez, the Spanish Foreign Minister, when presenting the Spanish programme had this in mind when he remarked that: 'The crisis looming over European integration has been overcome and we have stretching out before us a period of time in which we can work constructively without having to take decisions on what ought to be termed questions of survival' The *Official Journal of the EC*, Debates of the EP, 2–373, 17 January 1989, Office for Official Publications, Luxembourg, pp. 28–55.

27   At the Hannover European Council in June 1988 a committee was established which consisted of the governors of the twelve national banks and was chaired by Jacques Delors. It subsequently became known as the Delors committee.

28   Quoted in the *Official Journal of the EC*, Debates of the EP, 17 July 1989, Office for Official Publications, Luxembourg, p. 56.

29   Interviews with French government officials.

30   Jorgen G. Christensen goes as far as to argue that there is 'no realistic chance for a country of either setting its mark on the policies or determining the agenda of the Community'. Christensen, 'The Presidency of the Council of Ministers of the European Communities: the case of Denmark', in O Nuallain and Hoscheit, eds, *The Presidency of the European Council of Ministers*, p. 71.

31   For example, 1987 marked the thirtieth anniversary of the signing of the Treaties of Rome.

32   Such themes were: the European year for road safety (1986), the European year of the environment (1987), and the European cancer information year (1989).

33   See Werner Ungerer, 'EC Progress under the German Presidency', *Aussen Politik* (German foreign affairs review), XXXIX, 4, 1988, p. 321.

34   This was the view of a substantial number of government officials interviewed.

35   The French government had presented an eight point proposal at the Rhodes summit in December 1988. It also had held an audiovisual conference between 30 September and 2 October 1989 in Paris.

36   Whilst the Fontainebleau European Council of 1984 had made some temporary arrangement with regard to British budgetary rebates, by 1986–7 the limits of this arrangement had been reached.

37   In conjunction with the implementation of the February 1988 European Council decision, the Greek Presidency had made the design of working guidelines for the European Communities structural funds a main priority.

38   As part of the twenty-fifth anniversary of the Franco–German Friendship Treaty, the French government had tried to couple increased security co-operation with increased monetary co-operation and had proposed the establishment of an Economic Council.

39   Stage one of this 'report' called for full implementation of the internal market, closer co-ordination of member states' economic and monetary policies, abolition of exchange controls and entry by all member states into

the European Monetary System on equal terms. Stage two envisaged the establishment of a European System of Central Banks (ESCB), a narrowing of margins of fluctuations within the Exchange Rate Mechanism (ERM), a pooling of some exchange reserves and precise though not binding Community rules on national budget deficits and their financing. Stage three foresaw the ESCB establising a common monetary policy to replace co-ordinated independent national monetary policies, official reserves pooled and managed by the ESCB, decisions on exchange market interventions left to the ESCB, and irrevocably locked exchange rates, probably followed by the introduction of a single currency.

40   Statement by Roland Dumas, French Foreign Minister, before the EP, the *Official Journal of the EC*, Debates of the EP, 27 July 1989, Office for Official Publications, Luxembourg, p. 63.

41   See for example, Juliet Lodge, 'Social policy', *Journal of European Integration*. XIII, pp. 135–50; and Emil J. Kirchner, *Trade Unions as a Pressure Group in the European Community*, Westmead, 1977, chapter 7.

42   This social charter embraces employment/unemployment, health and safety at the workplace, vocational training, the rights and freedoms of employees and trade unions, equal treatment for men and women, and the protection of the environment.

43   Seveso marked the dioxin tragedy in 1986; drums containing Toxic waste were being transported within the Community without even the most elementary safety precautions.

44   See the statement by Delors before the EP, the *Official Journal of the EC*, Debates of the EP, 6 July 1988, Office for Official Publications, Luxembourg, p. 140.

45   For further details on the MFA see footnote 17 in chapter 3.

46   Troika is a system whereby three Presidencies liaise closely: the incumbent, the predecessor and the successor. It was first introduced with regard to EPC matters in 1981, in the so called London Report, and extended to internal market affairs in 1985.

47   H. Wallace, 'The Presidency of the Council of Ministers', p. 275.

48   For example, the Troika visited Israel, Egypt, Jordan and Syria, and met Yasser Arafat in Madrid.

49   Quoted in the *Official Journal of the EC*, Debates of the EP, 11 June 1986 Office for Official Publications, Luxembourg, p. 114.

50   This apparently was the wish of Jacques Delors. See Peter Hort, 'Der Europaeische Rat', Werner Weidenfeld and Wolfgang Wessels, eds, 1986–7, *Jahrbuch der Europaeischen Integration 1986/87*, Bonn, 1987, p. 54.

51   This was done successfully by Britain on its employment initiative, by France on proposals concerning the audiovisual sector, and by Spain on Monetary Union. Greece was less successful with regard to its initiative on social policy, even though Greece had sent a memorandum on this subject to the Commission three months in advance of its Presidency.

52   National co-ordinators are national representatives dealing exclusively with internal market matters within COREPER.

53   For details on 'A' and 'B' point procedures see chapter 3 of this book.

54   There have, however, been exceptions. For example, the informal

ECOFIN meeting at Nyborg, in November 1987, took a number of decisions to strengthen the EMS.

55   See Werner Ungerer, 'Die neuen Verfahren nach der Einheitlichen Europaeischen Akte: Eine Bilanz aus der Ratsperspektive' *Integration*, 3/89, Bonn, July 1989, p. 98.

56   For example, West Germany accepted being 'outvoted' with regard to the directive on machine tool in order, so it seemed, to demonstrate its inability to fulfil demands presented by the German machine tool lobby.

57   See Ungerer, 'Die neuen Verfahren', p. 98.

58   Quoted in the *Official Journal of the EC*, Debates of the EP, 7 February 1987, Office for Official Publications, Luxembourg, p. 27.

59   Ibid.

60   This compromise proposal consisted of a reduction in agricultural expenditures, (without questioning the basic principle of CAP), a substantial rise in regional aid, (but not as high as proposed by the Commission), and EC financial reforms.

61   This view was particularly held by Belgian government officials.

62   This compromise made two significant concessions to British demands for rigorous controls on farm spending. In other respects the proposals were rather coy, leaving many blanks to be filled in by the summiteers. But it made specific suggestions on aid to poorer regions, new ceilings on EC revenue of around 1.3% of the Community's GNP, on ceilings for cereal harvests, placing a limit on overall EC farm spending, and an offer to extend Britain's rebate.

63   Quoted in the *Official Journal of the EC*, Debates of the EP, 16 June 1988, Office for Official Publications, Luxembourg.

64   Only phase one of the Delors committee report was adopted at the Madrid European Council.

65   Quoted in the *Official Journal of the EC*, Debates of the EP, 26 July 1989, Office for Official Publications, Luxembourg, p. 56.

66   See, for example, the European Parliament debate of 6 July 1988. *Official Journal of the EC*, Debates of the EP, 6 July 1988, Office for Official Publications, Luxembourg, p. 144.

67   See Woyke, 'Belgien, Niederland, Luxemburg', p. 335.

68   See Peter Hort, 'Der Europaeische Rat', in Werner Weidenfeld and Wolfgang Wessels, eds, *Jahrbuch der Europaeischen Integration, 1988/89*, Bonn, 1989, p. 43.

69   Ibid., p. 45.

70   See Heinz-Juergen Axt, 'Griechenland', Weidenfeld and Wessels, eds, *Jahrbuch der Europaeischen Integration, 1988/89*, Bonn, 1989, p. 327.

71.   Guy de Bassompiere, *Changing The Guard in Brussels: An Insider's View of the EC Presidency*, New York, 1988, p. 81.

72   Consultation and co-operation is intensified before and during the Presidency and involves various levels: college, individual Commissioners, services on the Commission's part, and government members, government services, and the Permanent Delegation on the Presidency's part. Greece, France and West Germany had joint meetings between the government and the Commission college.

73   As Delors pointed out with regard to the Copenhagen summit: 'Failure is also failure of the Comission. When things go badly within Europe, every one is at fault'. Quoted in the *Official Journal of the EC*, Debates of the EP, 16 December 1987, Office for Official Publications, Luxembourg, p. 132.

74   The Stuttgart European Council of 1983 decided that the Presidency should report to the EP on the outcome of each European Council.

75   Karl Heinz Buck, 'Der Ministerrat', Weidenfeld and Wessels, eds, *Jahrbuch Europaeische Integration 1986/87*, Bonn, 1987, p. 63.

76   For further details on French position towards the EP see Chapter 6.

77   See Christensen, 'The Presidency of the Council of Ministers', p. 71.

78   Ibid.

79   H. Wallace and Edwards concluded in 1976 that: 'The only strategy left to the chair is to block issues by keeping them off the agenda or by delaying their discussion in Committee, except for the rare moment of good luck when a Presidency is able to claim credit for an agreement that was already on the books'. Helen Wallace and Geoffrey Edwards, 'European Community: the evolving role of the Presidency of the Council', *International Affairs*, October 1976, p. 549.

80   Quoted in the *Official Journal of the EC*, Debates of the EP, 16 December 1987, Office for Official Publications, Luxembourg, p. 127.

81   Poul Schluter, the Danish Prime Minister, complained that governments had not given their portfolio ministers enough discretion to enable them to complete their business in their own Council of Ministers meetings. See the *Official Journal of the EC*, Debates of the EP, 16 December 1987, Office for Official Publications, Luxembourg, p. 128.

82   As Jacques Delors remarked, the Hannover summit was 'reminiscent of the early days of informal discussions, so informal that it was a rarity to see leaders and foreign ministers reading from pre-prepared notes'. Quoted in the *Official Journal of the EC*, Debates of the EP, 6 July 1988, Office for Official Publications, Luxembourg, p. 140. For an anlysis of the original aims of the European Council see Gianni Bonvicini and Elfriede Regelsberger, 'The decision-making process in the EC's European Council', *The International Spectator*, XXII, 3, pp. 152–76.

83   I am indebted to John Fitzmaurice for having brought this point to my attention.

84   Guy de Bassompierre goes as far as to suggest that 'Presidency, however worthy and able can only influence, at best, 5 to 10 per cent of issues', de Bassompierre, *Changing the Guard*, p. 130.

85   H. Wallace, 'The Presidency of the Council of Ministers', p. 274.

86   O Nuallain and Hoscheit, *The Presidency of the European Council of Ministers*, p. XI.

6

The dynamics and agenda of EC decision-making

Introduction

The two Inter-governmental Conferences on Economic and Monetary Union (IGC-EMU) and on Political Union (IGC-PU) which were initiated in December 1990, signalled yet another milestone in the Community's history. As with the Single European Act (SEA), both the protagonists of integration and the defenders of the nation state could claim a degree of satisfaction. To proponents of neo-functionalism the progression from ECSC to EEC, SEA and the two new treaties that are envisaged is part of the cumulative logic of sectoral/functional spillover. Realists stress the continued control of national bodies or actors. These involve national finance ministers with regard to the projected common monetary policy, and heads of state or governments with regard to foreign and security matters. Realists also list the continued role of regulatory committees, composed of national representatives, which the SEA helped to sustain for the implementation of Council of Ministers decisions on internal market matters.

Closer examination reveals the inadequacies of the arguments of each protagonist. Yes, a sectoral expansion has taken place but this expansion is not driven by the actors singled out by the neo-functionalists, namely interest groups, political parties, and central bureaucracy (Commission).[1] It is governments and statesmen who decide on the pace and extent of co-operation. Moreover, whilst governments respond to economic pressures with greater co-operation, this does not confirm neo-functional assumptions of a prevailing continuum from economic to political integration. There were as many, if not more, political reasons (political situation in Eastern Europe and especially German re-unification) which set the stage for a treaty on political union. On the other hand, by engaging in progressive collective commitments in the political and security field, gradually relinquishing powers over monetary policy, and allowing more majority voting, member states are losing important controls over their national interest which may eventually affect their status as nation states. Governments therefore tread a treacherous path between increasing transnational co-operation (needed to fulfil important service functions for their citizens) and maintaining sufficient national control over EC decision-making. However, this national control is not the individual control of single governments but the control of national governments collectively. The role of the European Council and the Council Presidency take on great importance in this respect. Having become legitimised through the SEA, they can be seen as both contributors to, and beneficiaries of, the two new treaties that are envisaged.

The aim in this chapter is to assess whether the role of the Council Presidency, as well as that of the European Council, is still in the ascendancy or whether it is beginning to decline. This will be done by examining the implications of the two intergovernmental conferences on these two bodies, and by examining the likely agenda with which both will have to cope in the next few years. Points of discussion will involve the following. If more majority voting in the Council of Ministers occurs, how will that affect the role of the Presidency as a mediator? How will closer policy integration between European Political Co-operation (EPC) and EC external trade policy affect the relationship between the Commission and the Presidency? Will the democratic deficit be overcome by strengthening the powers of the EP, by reinforcing the role of national parliaments in EC decision-making, or by a combination of both? Another point of interest will be to compare the main differences and similarities in negotiations between the SEA and the two new treaties. The final section will deal with the future of the EC and the issue of 'deeper' versus 'wider'. It will also evaluate realism and neo-functionalism, in the light of both the empirical evidence gathered on the implementation of the SEA, the impact of the Presidency and developments surrounding the two IGCs. Mention will also be made of the future of integration and the nation state.

The dynamics of change

A number of primary and secondary factors can be identified as causes of the two IGCs. For both IGCs the impetus provided by the implementation of the SEA was a primary factor. Additional primary factors, specifically related to the IGC-PU were; (1) the regime changes in Eastern Europe at the end of 1989 and of German re-unification in 1990; (2) and, in the later phase of the preparation for the IGC-PU, the Gulf crisis. Secondary factors were (1) government actions and reactions, especially when used in conjunction with the holding of the EC Council Presidency; and (2) the role of the Commisssion, especially that of its president, Jacques Delors, and the contributions made to the debate by the EP. Whereas the SEA factor resembles the 'spillover logic' of neo-functionalism and comes from the internal dynamic of integration, the other primary factors originated from sources external to the integration process, which, as Bassompiere points out, have always spurred the EC on.[2] Due to the fact that these latter factors were unanticipated, their occurrence, and cumulative effect, caused a certain amount of 'overload' for the Community decision-making machinery.[3] Though these factors are separate in nature they overlap and are, to a large extent, mutually reinforcing. The following provides a brief description of these factors.

SEA dynamics
Since its inception in 1986, the SEA has been a continuous process which has been thought provoking a platform for economic growth. Through it, the EC has been able to move forward purposefully in terms of scope, jurisdiction, decision-making capacity, inter-institutional relations, and democratic accountability. The possibility of majority voting for many of the internal market provisions has resulted in quicker decisions and more effective action. The risk of being outvoted has discouraged member states from simply stalling in negotiation and has further reinforced the reluctance to use the veto. Both the success in the completion of the internal market programme and the link between this programme and policies in the regional, monetary, social, and external field have substantially expanded the scope of EC activities and the competences of the Commission. In part the link between the internal market programme and other policies stemmed from SEA commitments towards economic and social cohesion, towards convergence of economic and monetary policies, and towards efforts to maintain the technological and industrial conditions necessary for security. The

momentum of the internal market programme has highlighted the need for a social dimension; e.g. the awareness that the internal market would not be complete without a compensatory protection for workers, thus confirming, at least in part, the spillover logic of neo-functionalism. Through the SEA the role of EC law and the Court of Justice has been enhanced. With the co-operation and assent procedure the inter-institutional relationship has improved and the EP has become endowed with certain co-decision abilities, thereby reducing the prevailing democratic deficit in EC decision-making (see chapter 1). At the same time as the internal market programme moved ahead, pressure was building up within the Community to extend the powers of the EP and to reassess the Community's political role.[4] Finally, it should be remembered that the SEA's preamble renewed the commitment to European Union.

The SEA has exerted, and continues to exert, influence which goes far beyond the texts themselves. Rather than becoming the 'Euro-mouse' described by Spinelli (because it was all that remained of the EP's own treaty for European Union), it has become a significant landmark for the effectiveness of the EC. Whilst Sbragia suggests that the SEA represents a rough road map for closer political union,[5] Stanley Hoffmann goes even further to argue that what is at stake in the internal market programme is 'the future of the nation state in Western Europe'.[6] However, the SEA is only one element among many which are moving the Community towards a reassessment of its constitution and external role.[7]

Eastern Europe, Germany, and the Gulf
Regime changes in Eastern Europe in 1989 signalled the end of the Cold War period but also produced a climate of uncertainty and placed new political demands on existing alliances. German re-unification had raised diverse fears over a German tendency to neutrality, the possibility of dominance, and the German ability to contribute effectively towards EMU, because of the financial strain of re-unification. The Dutch were particularly outspoken, arguing that the main argument for political union was to bind the Germans into the EC while they were still willing.[8] Consequently, in early 1990 several EC member states, and the Commission, accelerated their call for closer European union, and for a European Germany rather than a German-dominated Europe. The beginning of the Gulf crisis, in August 1990, exposed the apparent EC dilemma of being an

economic giant but a political dwarf and stimulated further interest in both political union and a common foreign and security policy, i.e. the need to speak with one voice in the world. This sharpened the need, among other things, for the Community to overcome the existing demarcation between economic trade and foreign political issues, and to begin to treat foreign and security policy as a seamless whole.

Governments, the Presidency, and the Commission
Nonetheless, both the SEA, and the external factors (Eastern Europe, Germany, and the Gulf) have provoked different reactions among governments. It should be remembered that the SEA was a political compromise between the need to increase Community competences and the desire to maintain national control. Or put differently, some countries had seen the SEA as an end in itself with a heavy emphasis on the internal market component, whereas others had viewed it as a means to an end (European Union). Therefore, two related sets of questions began to affect the debate over the two IGCs in 1990. Firstly, whether it made sense for the existing Twelve to seek to accelerate its progress towards integration, or whether it should concentrate on fulfilling existing commitments centred on completing the internal market. Secondly, whether the prospect of Community enlargement should have priority over the deepening and solidifying of existing EC structures. Whereas the UK called for a pause and early association to help Eastern Europe as a higher priority, other member states and the Commission advocated a further qualitative advance by the Community before it has fully implemented the internal market programme.[9]

Of course the momentum towards EMU also stimulated discussions on Political Union, e.g. a perceived ongoing link from a common/single currency to a common/single economic and monetary policy and then to political union. Indeed, the Commission sees EMU as the motor behind political union. A point also made by the Germans who are adamant that there must be a link between the two, and therefore call for increased EP powers in EC decision-making. Equally, certain member states see EMU as an incentive to anchor Europe to Germany's low inflation rate and to build a single monetary system to fit the single market. It would also act as a means of sharing the decision-taking of the Bundesbank and locking the Federal Republic more firmly within the Community, or, as a way of diluting German dominance.

It is the Commission's duty to propagate Community objectives and it is natural to assume that the Commission seeks to expand its competences. By acting as its own lobby for further integration it collides with governments who resist further integration,[10] or who seek to tie increased co-operation with intergovernmental methods and thereby to maintain national control. The role of the Commission, and especially its President, requires a number of things which appear almost incompatible with each other: to purposely move the Community forward; effectively promote decision-making within the Council of Ministers through proposals which find broad support or avoid offending individual member states, and skilfully win the support of the EP, whilst maintaining the right to initiate and finalise proposals.

It is the first two aspects to which Delors has directed much of his energies. The unfolding of the SEA and the preparation of the two IGCs were carefully planned in four stages. Stage one occurred when Commissioner Cockfield proposed an administrative strategy for the internal market in 1985 with specific directives and specific dates which made the market project seem both comprehensible and manageable. Stage two was the introduction of the so-called Delors package in 1987 consisting of regional aid, and financial and agricultural reforms. This package put enormous strain on EC policy-makers before it was finally adopted in February 1988 during the German presidency. Stage three focused on EMU and centres on the April 1989 outline of a three-phase process presented by the so-called Delors committee.[11] However, the timing of each phase was left open. Stage four was an attempt to capitalise on the momentum created by the internal market programme, by the ongoing EMU discussions, and by the events in Eastern Europe and the Gulf, and to press for policy and institutional reforms through the October 1990 Commission proposal for political union.[12]

The role of the Commission's President is similar to that of the Council Presidency, except that the latter consists of several individuals, for example, the head of state or government, the foreign minister, or individual ministers of the country holding the six-monthly Presidency. As with the Commission President, it makes a difference which country or leaders are involved, though the short duration, largely predetermined agenda, and the Troika principle constrain the influence of the Council Presidency. It is advisable to distinguish between managerial role and role as innovator. The first is associated with such tasks as the implementation of the internal market programme. The second involves, for example, the attempted link between the internal market programme and other policies mentioned in the SEA (monetary, social, environmental, etc.), as well as initiatives in the external field, and measures to prepare for the two IGCs.[13] France was particularlyinnovative in 1989 in dealing with events in Eastern Europe by calling for an extraordinary European Council meeting; the Irish (with regard to German re-unification and the IGC-PU) and the Italians (with regard to the Gulf crisis and the IGC-PU) followed with similar arrangements. The Luxembourg Presidency was also innovative with the use of a questionnaire on a common foreign and security policy which it submitted to the foreign ministers before a Council meeting in February 1991.

Often the Commission and Council presidencies work closely together but occasionally the two are at loggerheads or pursue different objectives. An example of the latter occurred during the 1986 British Presidency (see Chapter 5). Though there are many examples of close working relationships, the 1988 German, 1989 French, and 1990 Italian Presidencies deserve particular mention. It would have been interesting had Britain been in charge of the Presidency during the 1989 and 1990 period when crucial decisions regarding the EMU, the Social Charter, and especially on political union were taken. Already in late 1990 Delors was pressing for a conclusion of the negotiations on the two IGCs during 1991, ahead of the next British Presidency by July 1992.

Presidents cannot blatantly pursue national interests. They must try to arbitrate amongst competing interests and seek to carry at least a majority of member states. Mediating and building packages is thus one of the main tasks of a Presidency. The Italian Presidency of 1990 can be seen in this light. Determined to quicken the pace of both IGCs, the Italians kept GATT discussions on farm prices to a minimum, in part to avoid a British diversionary tactic[14], and in part to avoid alienating France and Germany, two of the hardliners on GATT negotiations. The Italians infuriated Mrs Thatcher, who felt outwitted for the second time by an Italian Presidency and under similar circumstances.[15] For their part, the Italians denied that they had deliberately tried to ambush Thatcher.[16] However, after the Rome European Council, the Dutch also accused the Italian Presidency of having adopted conclusions on the future role of the European Council, which they argued went beyond the so-called 'agreed results' of the leaders present.[17]

The negotiations

Arrangements for the two IGCs were made with regard to EMU at the European Council meetings in Madrid (June 1989), Strasbourg (December 1989), and Rome (December 1990), and on Political Union at the European Council meetings in Dublin (April and June 1990) and in Rome (October and December 1990). Proceedings for both conferences were to be conducted according to Article 236 of the Rome Treaty, under which a simple majority would be sufficient to invoke such a conference, but any decision arising from it with a view to revising the treaties must be adopted unanimously. Negotiations were to be concluded by the end of 1991, ratified by national parliaments in 1992,[18] and the new treaties were to come into force in 1993.

With regard to EMU, proceedings became affected by German attemps to forge an economic and monetary union in the summer of 1990, as part of the process towards German re-unification. However, there appeared to be sufficient cohesion among the member states, with the exception of Britain, that the three-stage proposal, laid out in the Delors Report, should be followed vigorously. In contrast Britain, which opposed stages two and three of the Delors plan – a single currency, a single monetary policy, and irrevocably fixed exchange rates – had proposed a 'hard ECU' as a possible stepping stone towards EMU.[19] What remained unclear also, in the beginning of 1991, was how the German (Bundesbank's) insistence on the independence of the European Central Bank could be reconciled with the British view that the interests of governments must be predominant in monetary affairs.

The Dublin summit in June invited national governments, the Commission and the EP to make contributions to the preparatory work to be carried out by the foreign ministers on the IGC-PU. However, by that time the Belgian government had already introduced a memorandum in which it stated the reasons why moves towards Political Union had become necessary, and in which it proposed three broad reforms: reinforcing the institutions to make their interaction more efficient; increasing the democratic element by strengthening the EP; and bringing together EPC and Community policies, in particular with respect to Eastern Europe. This proposal provoked a sarcastic remark from the British Foreign Minister, Douglas Hurd, that Belgium had been the first to dive into the swimming pool, even though there was no water in it. The governments of Greece, Spain and Italy subsequently introduced their memoranda echoing the main tenets of the Belgian proposals and stressing the need for co-operation in foreign and security policy. Though Belgium, Greece and Italy had raised the issue of fundamental rights and freedoms, Spain put the case more explicitly by suggesting European citizenship. This was to involve: civil rights (participation in elections to the EP in the country of residence, and possible participation in municipal elections); social and economic rights (freedom of movement and residence irrespective of engagement in economic activity, and equality of opportunity and of treatment for all of Community citizens); and cultural exchange and education. In turn, the EP and the Commission presented their views in the autumn of 1990. Finally, shortly before the Rome European Council meeting in December 1990, the French and German governments introduced their recommendations. Consequently, by the time of the December summit, all member states, except Britain, were 'on record' as wishing to see the Community become a political union.[20] The British view was to do as little as possible on institutional reform, and to prevent an extension of the Commission's competences, majority voting in the Council of Ministers, and EP legislative powers. There were, however, substantial differences on points of detail within the group favouring expansion. The debate centred on the scope of policies which should come under Community jurisdiction and the form of decision-making which should be used in the adoption of these policies. In particular, foreign and security policy became a main focus of attention. Another controversial point arose over the extent to which an increase of the powers of the EP should take place.

The eleven countries agreed generally that renewed efforts should be made both for achieving the aims stipulated in the SEA (with regard to, for example, fiscal, social,[21] cohesion, environmental and research policy), and that fresh proposals should be introduced to cover consumer protection, health, education, culture, energy, major networks and border control issues. The latter was also to relate to immigration, visas, asylums, drugs, and organised crime. Disagreement prevailed, however, over the form of decision-making for these policies. Whereas nine of the eleven favoured majority voting on these policies, (with Germany favouring additional special voting rights for social laws),[22] Ireland expressed reservations over the use of majority voting with regard to social laws.[23] Luxembourg opposed the extension of majority voting to any new subjects, except for social laws and the environment and particularly wanted to protect the unanimity rule on tax matters.[24]

Whilst all countries (including Britain) favoured closer co-operation in the foreign and security field, as table 6.1 shows, only seven wanted to see parts of this accompanied by majority decision-making; two additional countries (Ireland and Luxembourg) were ambivalent. Common security was to deal with questions of arms control, disarmament and related issues; CSCE matters; certain questions debated in the UN, including peace-keeping operations; economic and technological co-operation in the armaments field;[25] co-ordination of armaments export policy, and nuclear non-proliferation. Defence should be considered without prejudice to member states' existing obligations in this area, and should bear in mind the importance of ties with the Atlantic alliance without pre-judicing the traditional position of other member states. However, most difficulties arose over how far co-operation should go. For example, should the areas of common interest be identified before and written into the new treaty; could member states reserve the right to pursue national interest separately and should a defence component be added to security policy. Equally, should co-operation include an organic link between WEU and EC; should the European Council rather than the Commission be mainly in charge; and how far might democratic control be exercised in decision-making. Two diametrically opposed positions emerged between the French and the Benelux. According to the French view, which also re-appeared in the joint French–German report in December 1990, the European Council would set broad policy strategy, the Council of Ministers would work out policy details, and the Commission would get the right to propose foreign policy iniatives (though not to the exclusion of national proposals, as with normal EC business). To facilitate the link between Community policies and EPC, the EPC secretariat would be merged with the Council of Ministers' secretariat. Under these proposals the EP powers would not be increased much. A congress of MEPs and national MPs would give opinions on foreign policy and economic and monetary union. The

European Council would decide, by unanimous vote, which areas of
foreign policy to treat as common and decisions in some of those
areas would then be taken by majority vote.[26] The Benelux opposed
the use of the European Council in this way, arguing that small
countries lose out when heads of state and government dominate.
They preferred instead to strengthen the role of the Commission,
who they see as their protector. Naturally, the French position was
also perceived as a threat by the Commission.

Table 6.1 *Countries' position held in late 1990*

	Favours majority voting in some parts of foreign policy	Favours eventual EC–WEU fusion	Favours more powers for the EP on EC law
Belgium	yes	yes	yes
Denmark	no[a]	no	yes
France	yes	yes	no
Germany	yes[b]	yes	yes
Greece	yes	yes	yes
Ireland	maybe[c]	no	no
Italy	yes	yes	yes
Luxembourg	maybe	yes	no
Netherlands	yes	no	yes
Portugal	yes[d]	maybe	no
Spain	yes	yes	yes
United Kingdom	no	no[e]	no[f]

Source: Adopted and modified from the *Economist*, 1 December 1990.
Notes:
[a] Afraid majority voting would make it harder for its Nordic neighbours,
some of which are neutrals, to join the EC.
[b] Nonetheless Germany is cautious and does not want to undermine
NATO, or offend the Americans (and possibly the Russians). Similar
reservations are, of course, expressed by Britain.
[c] Accepts the aims of a common foreign and security policy but insists that
defence should be left to NATO and the WEU.
[d] Suggests, however, that all countries big or small, have one vote each (in
contrast to the weighted voting).
[e] However, Britain favours closer links between the two.
[f] However, Britain calls for a public-accounts committee, to monitor EC
spending.

With the exception of the British, Danish, Dutch and Irish, the
Franco–German proposal for a step by step integration of WEU into
the EC and the forging of single EC positions in NATO and the UN

Security Council had the support of the other six member states. Britain, whilst in favour of strengthening WEU, supported Dutch concern that the Americans remain closely involved in European security.[27] However, in their December 1990 joint declaration, Kohl and Mitterrand also stressed that Europe's new security arrangements should strengthen NATO.[28] Moreover, whereas France, Italy and Spain suggested that Article 5 of the WEU treaty, which obliges members to help each other if attacked, should be written into the EC treaty, Britain was opposed to this. Italy had also proposed a common deployment of EC forces, e.g. peace keeping operations under UN mandates.

The involvement of the EP in foreign and security policy formation was one of the suggestions put forward in the Belgian and in the Italian memorandum. According to this, the General Affairs Council, consisting of the foreign ministers, would be primarily in charge of such matters and would consider proposals either from the Commission or the EP. This brings into focus the general question as to whether the powers of the EP should be increased and, if so, in which areas, to what extent and under which procedure.

Two opposing views emerged between the Dutch and Italians on the one hand, and the French and the British on the other over the granting of further powers to the EP. Both the Dutch and the Italians were unwilling to ratify a new treaty unless the EP got important legislative powers,[29] with the Italians insisting that the EP should get as much say on laws as the Council of Ministers. A strengthening of the EP's legislative powers, a widening of the co-operation and assent procedure, and a decisive role in the investiture of the Commission was also demanded by Belgium, Germany, Greece and Spain. In contrast, France believed that as the Community takes on powers in new areas, national governments and parliaments should play a greater role than in some of the existing areas. Accordingly, the European Council would report to a grand assembly composed of MEPs and MPs, which would meet twice a year. With regard to the co-operation procedure, however, the French recommended that the Commission should be excluded from further proceedings once the EP had amended a text; in such circumstances the Council alone would accept or reject its changed text. Importantly also the joint Franco–German declaration also grants the EP the right to confirm, by vote, the appointment of both the president of the Commission and, at a later stage, all the Commissioners. All member states (including Britain) seemed to favour increased EP powers on budget control and financial accountability, and a closer monitoring by the EP of the implementation of Community policies.

The Commission was apprehensive about extensive legislative rights for the EP, seeing its own rights of initiation and mediation in jeopardy. It was also unhappy over a British, Danish and Spanish proposal which envisaged the sacking of individual Commissioners by the EP, arguing that this would undermine the Commission's 'collegial spirit'. On the other hand, Delors would like to have power over fellow Commissioners, the right to veto a member state's choice of Commissioner, and the power to change a Commissioner's portfolio.

As with any negotiation, optimising preferred options is difficult to achieve and often has to be substituted with satisfying.[30] Often, therefore, what is achieved is what is possible under the circumstances rather than what is desirable or preferable. Package deals are one of the important means member states use as a satisfying strategy in the pursuit of national interest. These packages themselves are built on coalitions among like-minded governments and often involve trade-offs or side-payments.[31] The formation of coalitions can be fostered through the arbitration or mediation function of the Council Presidency. Bilateral co-operation is also an important means in this respect. This became visible in the French attempt to rouse British interest in the IGC–PU through a proposed strengthening of Anglo–French defence co-operation and an augmentation of WEU.[32] Equally, there were German efforts to combine the French desire for enhancing the role of the European Council with increasing the powers of the EP.

Whilst the EC is woven deeply into the economic fabric of its members and has definite bearings on the negotiations among the twelve member states, the issues involved in the proposed new treaties have significant implications for national sovereignty. Governments have to decide whether to surrender powers over the issuing of monies and the making of their own foreign and defence policies. There is hesitancy, therefore, not only by the British, but also on the part of the French (worries about control of the EC), the Germans (worries about the stability of the ECU), and the Dutch (worries about large state dominance). On the other hand, in October 1990 Kohl confirmed that acceleration was indeed the aim, and Mitterrand insisted that progress on European integration would not be dictated by the slowest.

The Principle of Subsidiarity

Whilst in the SEA negotiations the internal market programme acted as a catalyst, especially for countries like Britain, the absence of such an 'economic incentive' should not automatically be seen as impeding progress in the 1991 negotiations. Besides the threat of exclusion which might confront a country like Britain, a new element has emerged which has the potential to provide an essential ingredient for the further construction of both EMU and political union. This element is the principle of subsidiarity and relates to the allocation of competences between national and Community institutions.

Subsidiarity is not a new concept and, as J. Jacque and J. Weiler point out, is the cornerstone of all federalism, old and new. It is the principle whereby defence and foreign policy are granted to the central power and education and some social matters to the constitutent units.[33] Marc Wilke and Helen Wallace describe it as being shorthand for a cluster of issues about the sharing of powers at different levels of government in Western Europe.[34]

Subsidiarity is not new to the Community either. It finds expression in many facets of the existing Community order such as Article 235, the practice of 'mutual recognition' in harmonisation measures, and the instrument of the Directive.[35] The EP Draft Treaty for European Union makes reference to subsidiarity by stating that:

The Union shall only act to carry out those tasks which might be undertaken more effectively in common than by the member states acting separately, in particular those whose execution requires action by the Union because their dimension or effects extend beyond national frontiers.[36]

Whilst this reference put the emphasis on the transnational implications, the notion of subsidiarity first emerged officially in the SEA treaty with regard to environmental policies.

Various reasons can be cited why subsidiarity has come more into focus. These concern German Laender challenge, especially over the Television Broadcasting Directive;[37] fears of EC over-extension or overload, (the possibility of being outvoted makes member states more sensitive to the issue of where the legal powers to act are located by EC authorities); and the desire by the member states to retain rights in relation to the collectively exercised power of the Community as a whole.

As the Report of the House of Commons pointed out, subsidiarity is a political rather than a legal term. As a term it does not have any binding force unless given a legal definition, perhaps by treaty and subject to interpretation by the European Court of Justice. But, it is difficult to see how this could be easily achieved. Taken in one sense subsidiarity could be a powerful decentralising concept if properly defined and enforced, but on other definitions it will allow for greater centralisation.[38] We need to clarify, therefore, whether:[39]

1 *The private or the public sphere should control.* For example, important parts of the Social Charter could be left to the social partners and, to that extent, official rules and regulations (of a national and Community nature) could be dispensed with. In other words the private sphere would be given maximum leeway. Governments should interfere only where necessary;

2 *The local, regional or central government level is in charge.* This must be decided by each member state for itself in accordance with national law. For centralised countries, like Britain and France, this would mean that central bodies would only be allowed to take charge of tasks that cannot be handled sub-centrally;

3 *The Community level should regulate.* Here, the difficulty is whether to include articles on subsidiarity in the text or in the preamble of the new treaties. If the former route is adopted it would make it justiciable and presumably the direct subject of cases before the EC and the courts of the member states, e.g. whether to allow member states to appeal to the European Court of Justice if they consider that a Community decision exceeds the Community's powers as defined by the principle. The explicit insertion into the new treaty, which would obviously strengthen the role of the Court of Justice, was advocated by Germany, the Netherlands, and the UK. Most other countries seemed to prefer that it was merely mentioned in the preamble or an annexed document to the treaty. There is also the question of whether the Community needs its own subordinate authorities to administer the internal market, e.g. in the field of competition, health protection, environment, etc. The following possibilities could be considered:[40]

1 Article 100A and 235[41] could be amended since they are, in their current formulation, too open-ended.

2 The Council of Ministers could first take a decision in principle (in response to a Commission proposal) on legislating in an area of disputed, or potential, new competence and only then deal with Commission proposals on the substantive issue,
3 To have certain Community decisions/legislation endorsed by national parliaments.
4 To obtain a ruling from the Court of Justice in advance of relevant (or challenged) draft legislation becoming adopted finally.
5 To draw up categories in the treaty on political union, spelling out: what are exclusive Community powers, exclusive member state powers, and areas of concurrent powers. The latter category might be the longest list and would have to cover economic, industrial, social, fiscal and environmental policies, education and cultural matters and citizens rights.

Each of these possibilities has certain merits and a combination of them is likely to be adopted. The subsidiarity principle might therefore, ensure that member states retain what is needed to remain sovereign under international law, namely, the power to regulate law and order at home and preserve sufficient scope for independence in foreign and defence policies. Accordingly, the intensity of action at the Community level could be kept as low as possible so as to leave maximum room for manoeuvre to the member states. Further use of the principle of mutual recognition in harmonisation of laws would therefore maximise the practice of subsidiarity as would the reliance on minimum standards (insofar as the principles of the internal market allow this).[42]

How would the principle of subsidiarity work under the envisaged EMU? What responsibilities should a European Central Bank assume? Which operations may be left with the central banks of the Twelve? In the following, the institutional aspects and operational details in the envisaged monetary co-operation will be examined from the vantage point of the subsidiarity principle.

What is proposed is a European System of Central Banks consisting of the European Central Bank (ECB) and the national central banks, which would be known as the 'System'. This System would allow for central authority whilst ensuring an element of national control in decision-making. Its main decision-making bodies would be the Council of the Banks, and the executive board. The former would consist of the six members of the executive board and the governors of the national central banks. It would have the exclusive right to authorise the issue of notes within the Community, to formulate monetary objectives, to determine key interest rates, and to decide on the supply of reserves within the Community. Members of the executive board would consist of a president, a vice-president and four members, who would be appointed for eight years by the European Council, after consultation with the Council of Ministers and the EP. This board would be entrusted with the daily execution of monetary policies. Voting within these two main decision-making bodies would take place by majority with each member having one vote. The President of the ECB would attend meetings of the Council of Ministers which deals with financial matters, and one finance minister and a Commissioner would attend meetings of the ECB's Council. Independence would be secured in that neither the ECB nor a national central bank nor any members of their decision-making bodies may seek or take any instructions from Community institutions, governments of member states or any other body. However, there would be a question over the degree of independence of the executive board, i.e. should it be dependent on the Council of Banks. In addition, it is not clear what relationship would emerge between the ECB and the national monetary authorities. In line with the principle of subsidiarity two possible working methods could emerge. One would allow national central banks to execute operations arising out of the system's tasks. Under the other the executive board would be instructed to make use of the national central banks, whenever possible and appropriate, in the execution of its daily activities. Another remaining question involves the degree of independence the executive board would have vis-a-vis the Council of the Banks, e.g. the degree to which it could issue instructions to the national banks in its daily execution of monetary policy? What seems most likely is that exchange-rate policies (medium-term exchange-rate differentials, devaluations and evaluations) remain the responsibility of the Council of Ministers. On the other hand, member states would be expected to ensure that their national legislation, including the statutes of national central banks, would be compatible with the provisions of the new treaty and the EEC treaty. Member states would regard their conjunctural policies as a matter of common concern and would consult each other and the Commission on the relevant measures to be taken. The French envisaged strict rules forbidding member states from running up excessive budget deficits. It is unclear whether any sanctions could or should be issued against countries which run unauthorised budget deficits and, if sanctions were used, what form they should take. For example, should the Council of Ministers refuse to provide loans (or transfer payments) to such countries?

Under the proposal of the bank governors, the ECB would be consulted regarding draft Community legislation and new international agreements in the monetary, prudential, banking or financial field. In accordance with Community legislation, the ECB would be consulted by national authorities regarding any draft legislation within its field of competences. Annually, the ECB would draw up a report on the activities of the System and on the monetary policy and present it to the EC, the Council of Ministers and the EP.

In its December 1990 Draft Treaty on EMU, the Commission makes provisions for its own role. Accordingly, it wants to submit multi-annual guidelines on EMU to the European Council, which should discuss them after consultation with the EP. In line with these discussions, the Council of Ministers should decide on the adjustments that need to be made by individual countries to the multi-annual guidelines. In turn the Commission, together with the relevant EP committee, would be involved in the implementation of these adjustments.

The ultimate goal of EMU is to irreversibly lock exchange rates between participating Community currencies and to subsequently issue a single currency which will replace the present currencies. Two transitional stages are envisaged, in line with the three stages proposed in the Delors Report. The beginning of 1994 will mark the start of stage two, with the establishment of the System. In other words, the Community and the member states should have taken all the appropriate measures[43] at that stage to set up the various bodies and to allow the system to operate. Between 1994 and 1997, the Council of the Banks should report to the European Council on the result obtained and in particular on the progress achieved on convergence. On the basis of such reports and after consulting the EP, the European Council shall establish that the conditions for moving to the final stage have been met.

Essential to the success of these monetary plans is that they will be matched by economic policy co-ordination. However, uncertainty remains over how to control budget deficits, how to establish transfer payments to states with economic difficulties, or how to introduce sanctions if deviations occur in economic performance among the member states.

Whilst important questions remained unsettled on the treaty concerning EMU, there was also a lively debate about some of the central decision-making features of the envisaged treaty for Political Union, especially over how far the European Council's role should be accentuated. For example, the Dutch Premier, Ruud Lubbers, had raised doubts as to whether European Political Union could be established from the top down. The French proposal for vesting most of the powers in either the Council of Ministers or the European Council bore striking similarities to France's presidential system and seemed to reflect earlier French attempts for a political directorate at EC level; (consisting of Britain, France and Germany.)

This raised questions as to whether the European Council would become an over-cumbersome legal organ and whether it could retain its fundamental role of impetus and political guidance? Already there was a trend for the European Council to act as a kind of appeal court for the Council of Ministers.[44] Such a trend, if reinforced, could result in a slowing down of the normal legislative process. It could also sustain, at least to a substantial extent, the control of national governments over EC decision-making. Against that, a wider use of majority voting, as provided by the SEA, will be a counter weight. Will that also hold for the role of the Council Presidency? Firstly, if an increasing number of principal decisions, especially on EMU and on foreign and security policy, were to be taken at European Council level, the role of the Presidency might grow in influence and in its mediating function. In contrast, if the Council of Ministers is empowered, and able, to take most of these decisions largely by majority voting, then the mediating role of the Presidency might decline. However, under the latter scenario the Presidency's managerial/administrative role would probably still increase. In any case, the Presidency would retain its innovative role to link policy areas and create new policy agendas.

Moreover, it is reasonable to expect that the future will entail a closer sharing of workloads between the Commission and the Council Presidency on foreign policy. This would be the product of the overlap between external trade issues and foreign policy objectives on, for example, export of arm products or products of 'dual use' like electronics, chemicals or nuclear reactors. This might elevate the role and influence of the Commission, raise its profile and allow it to be involved in important Community decisions.

The same might not hold for the EP and the 'democratic deficit'. But some relief will occur by increasing powers to the EP, a more involved role of national (possibly also regional) parliaments, and through measures for the establishment of a 'European citizenship'. On the fundamental issue of the power balance between the Council of Ministers and the EP, as well as on the EP as a legislator, not much change is to be expected.

The Future of the nation state

The Community has not evolved into either a fully fledged supra-national body with strong central institutions nor into a federation with a constitutional order. However, as Sbragia suggests, it has had stunning success in establishing comparatively strong institutions to which its constituent units peacefully submit.[45] With each step towards closer union, the adjustments for member states becomes greater, but states will jealously continue to try to preserve their own special interests as far as possible. The limits or constraints to states defending their own national interests, or for that matter retaining a reasonable degree of control over EC decision-making, will depend on a number of items which are on the Community agenda for the next few years. Some of these are externally inspired, for example, the Gulf conflict, developments in the Soviet Union, (especially with regard to the ethnic issue), and the United States' position towards European defence and unification. Others are dependent on the degree of convergence, cohesion and mutual responsiveness member states can muster amongst themselves in establishing EMU, political union, (especially with regard to a common foreign and security policy), and in combining a deepening of integration with an enlarging of the Community. It is helpful to distinguish between common and single approaches to monetary or foreign/security policy. A common policy is an area in which member states agree to a joint effort while reserving the right to pursue national interests separately.

There was great concern in early 1991 that the disarray amongst member states over the handling of the Gulf conflict[46] had damaged prospects for political union and affected developments on the EMU negotiations.[47] The failure of the Twelve to speak with one voice had raised doubts as to whether the Community would be able to take joint actions. It had called into question the Franco–German attempt to strengthen the Community's role in the external field, had further escalated the suspicion of smaller countries over the proposed role of the European Council in foreign and security policies, and strengthened the British resolve to oppose measures towards a single currency, monetary policy, majority voting and EP powers. The American disenchantment with the lack of coherent European support was expected to result in a more rapid and extensive withdrawal of American troops from Europe (thus leaving an immediate security vacuum for the Europeans to fill). In addition, there was the prospect of pressure for the establishment of a European pillar within NATO, greater burden-sharing in the handling of international conflicts; and less American leniency in GATT negotiations over European agricultural subsidies.

If these concerns were not grave enough, the use of force by the Soviet authorities in the Baltic region in January 1991 added yet another layer of concern and urgency. Whilst it raised concerns over the stability of the Soviet Union and the prospects for its co-operation with the Community, it also provoked German anxiety over the remaining 300,000 Soviet troops still stationed in the eastern part of Germany, e.g. whether they could remain there if the Soviet Union re-emerged as a militarily inclined country. Such a potential could either be linked with the continued presence of American troops and the continued existence of NATO, or with the possibility of Germany seeking its own deal with the Soviet Union and pursuing a policy of neutrality. In any case, these events posed painful questions for the Germans over whether to stop finacial aid to the Soviet Union, or to increase its financial commitment to the Gulf War. This coincided with the enormous financial burden of German re-unification, the groundswell of pacifist feelings (as elsewhere in Western European countries), the spectre of having to raise taxes, and the anchor role of the Bundesbank within the EMS to ensure stable interest rates and exchange rates. Besides these concerns confronting the Community, there was also an element of urgency in how to prepare for the post-war Gulf situation, how to sustain commitments for the completion of the internal market programme by 1992, how to proceed effectively and energetically with the two IGCs, how to avoid a two-speed Community emerging as a consequence of introducing EMU,[48] and how to deal with such diverse applicants as Turkey (who had played an important role in that Gulf conflict), Austria, Cyprus and Malta. For example, far-reaching security policy implications might defer certain neutrals, like Austria or Sweden, from joining the Community. In the end most of the concerns come back to the central issue which has plagued the European integration enterprise, namely, how to achieve a sufficient degree of mutual trust, responsiveness or solidarity amongst its participating states. Thus, national concerns and national interests will continue to be a dominant feature in EC developments. At the same time states will be confronted with an ever-growing degree of interdependence, communication and inter-action and will find it increasingly difficult to thrive as fully independent economies.[49]

Integration: theory and practice

It is lamentable but a fact that after forty years of so-called integration in Western Europe no single theory has emerged which can explain these developments adequately and/or lend itself easily to predict the future of the EC. Neo-functionalism captures much of the internal dynamics, e.g. how much and why the EC has moved on from the ECSC to the EEC, the SEA and the two new IGCs. Neo-functionalism explains and predicts only part of these developments because it emphasises the role of interest groups and central bureau-cracy (mainly the Commission) at the expense of governments or statesmen; it emphasises the dependence among Community members and neglects the global interdependence of member states; it stresses the economic aspects rather than the political or security ones, and concentrates on the transfer of competences from the national to the Community level (zero sum model) rather than on joint tasks between the two levels. Neo-functionalism is unable: (1) to deal with the impact of personalities like De Gaulle or Thatcher; (2) to explain why the Community forsook solidarity in the mid-1970s and became dynamic in the mid-1980s; and (3) to assimi-late in its conceptual framework the thawing of the Cold War, the emergence of a re-unified Germany, and the growing pressure on West European countries to look after their own security. Realism, on the other hand, by focusing on the nation state as the unit of analysis, and stressing stability and security as major considerations, has been able to explain the pace of co-operation among West European countries, how bipolarity, for a long period, impeded EC integration efforts, and why West European states pursue global rather than solely EC strategies. But by insisting on the nation state as a unitary actor, it neglects the cross-cutting ties created by multi-national firms, interest groups, or such specialised agencies as the German Bundesbank. Equally, by putting emphasis on national control and by emphasising that states will forego economic benefits derived from international cooperation if long-term security interests are at risk, EC constraints on member state autonomy are unduly minimised. This is particularly relevant with regard to the potential implications for national sovereignty which the estab-lishment of a single EC currency would entail. Thus realists tend to treat the EC more as an appendage rather than as a constraint of national interest.

Until the mid-1980s, EC institutional integration did not proceed steadily and incrementally, as predicted by neo-functionalism. Rather, it went in fits and starts, more in accordance with inter-governmentalism, and decision-making was centred in the Council of Ministers and the European Council, (again, like inter-govermentalism), rather than towards the authority of the Commis-sion and EP, as neo-functionalism would predict.[50] However, the move from the SEA to the IGC–EMU was not only relatively quick, but seemingly reflected a steady and incremental development analo-gous to the spillover and forward linkage predicted by neo-functionalism. EC institutional momentum, (in the form of the success of the internal market programme), and the political leader-ship of the Commission President were at least partly responsible for the timing, content and process of negotiating the IGC–EMU.[51] The other part of this success rests with the acts of governments, pri-marily that of France and Germany, and is also reflected in the conduct of the Council Presidency, especially the German, Spanish and French between 1988 and 1989. More government impact can be expected in the actual IGC–EMU negotiations. Here different national positions have to be aggregated, e. g. whether to have a common or a single currency, whether the ECB should be completely independent or subject to some poltical control by governments, and whether or not the EP should have an element of control in the running of an EC monetary policy. Thus the outcome appears, once again, akin to the 'splitting of differences', as outlined in the decision-making model in chapter 1, rather than with a problem-solving or optimal policy-making solution. The same process is likely to apply for the IGC–PU.

In short, neither realism nor neo-functionalism adequately explains or predicts the collaborative efforts of EC member states. Neither, for that matter, does federalism, though the status of Community law as 'supreme', the 'direct effect' of EC law on national legislation, and the increasing use of the subsidiarity principle, demonstrate that this theory has some explanatory value. In the absence of an adequate theory, it might be useful to concentrate on how and why joint tasks emerge between member states and Community institutions and to use the analogy of how and why federalist states pursue joint tasks. Such joint tasks can be described as co-operative federalism, and signify that sovereignty is not an absolute concept, but rather one where a pooling of sovereignties is taking place. In such an analysis the decision-making process is the main focus. Such a focus analyses the main actors like governments (via the European Council, the Council of Ministers, or COREPER), the Council Presidency, the Commission and the EP, and it also considers the main procedures like voting by majority in the Council of Ministers, or the co-operation and assent procedures involving the EP. In turn, such an analysis helps to shed light on Scharpf's dichotomy between bargaining and problem solving and between optimal and sub-optimal policy making outcomes.

Conclusion

In substantive terms the EC has made considerable strides over time as reflected in the number of treaties (ECSC, EEC, SEA and the two IGCs) and in the geographic expansion from six to twelve. The same cannot be said in procedural terms. With the arrival of the Luxembourg Compromise in the mid-1960s, EC decision-making remained largely the domain of the member states, operated mostly according to either the principle of the lowest common denominator or the splitting of differences (rather than problem-solving). Institutions, like the Commission and the EP were kept in a subservient role vis-a-vis the Council of Ministers or the European Council. However, the Court of Justice was effective in expanding the supremacy of Community law. Governments, through the device of the European Council, Technical Councils, COREPER, the Council Presidency, and Regulatory Committees ensured that national control prevailed over important EC decisions. The EC modified its decision-making procedures for a number of reasons; partly due to the weight of a complex network of decision-making machinery (between COREPER, the Council of Ministers and the European Council, as well as the Commission), and partly due to the convergence of interests among EC member states which emerged over economic liberalisation in the beginning of the 1980s. In addition there were pressures of international competitiveness, and the need to prepare for the consequences of EC enlargement. Significantly, this allowed for limited majority voting, a certain amount of co-decision by the EP, (via the co-operation and assent procedure), a strengthening of the Commission's right to initiate legislation, and a streamlining of the Court of Justice's workload. The two IGCs envisage a strengthening of these decision-making procedures. They can be considered as yet another quantum leap forward. However, this leap has to be seen in the context of the important challenges facing the Community. The completion of the internal market by the end of 1992, the danger of another economic recession, the question of further enlargement, the need to reconcile more democracy with greater efficiency, and the shouldering of international responsibility are just some of the items on the agenda.

Notes

1 For an assessment of the actors and conceptual framework of neo-functionalism see Ernst B. Haas, *The Uniting of Europe: Political, Social, and Economic Forces, 1950–1957*, Stanford, 1958.

2 Guy de Bassompierre, *Changing the Guard in Brussels: An Insider's View of the Presidency*, New York, 1988, p. 126.

3 Besides being occupied with the two IGCs, events in Eastern Europe, Germany, and the Gulf, the EC was involved in negotiations with GATT (Uruguay Round) and EFTA, and was engaged with the CSCE dialogue.

4 See Shirley Williams, 'Sovereignty and accountability in the European Community', *Political Quarterly*, LXI, 3, 1990, p. 311.

5 Alberta Sbragia, 'The European Community and institutional development: politics, money and law', paper presented to the Brookings Institution's conference on European political institutions and policymaking after 1992, 29–30 March 1990, p. 1.

6 Stanley Hoffmann, 'What is at stake is the future of the nation state in western Europe', *European Affairs*, fall 1989, p. 41.

7 See House of Commons Foreign Affairs Committee, Second Report on The Operation of the Single European Act, Session 1989–90, 14 March 1990.

8 See the *Economist*, 1 December 1990.

9 See House of Commons Foreign Affairs Committee, Second Report on

The Operation of the Single European Act.

10   Among the instances where Jacques Delors collided with British Prime Ministers were his announcement in July 1988 that in ten years time 80 per cent of economic affairs would be decided by EC institutions, and his remark at the end of the European Council meeting in Rome in December 1990 that he was 'distrustful of the British approach'.

11   For details on the Delors Committee Report, see footnote 39 in chapter 5.

12   'Commission Opinion of 21 October 1990 on the Proposal for Amendment of the Treaty Establishing the European Economic Community with a View to Political Union', COM(90) 600 final, Brussels, 23 October 1990.

13   Examples of innovative Presidencies include Germany finalising the Delors package, and launching monetary co-operation efforts; Greece and Spain promoting social policy efforts; France reinforcing efforts in the monetary and social field, and responding to events in Eastern Europe; Ireland paving the way for the IGC–PU, and together with Italy making provisions for German reunification; Italy dealing with economic sanctions against Iraq, commencing talks on associate membership with Poland, Hungary and Czechoslovakia, and, importantly, preparing the opening of the two intergovernmental conferences on EMU and political union.

14   Britain had tried to use the European Council primarily for overcoming the deadlock over GATT negotiations. It probably would have also liked to demonstrate that this apparent disunity was yet another reason why no further steps towards political union should be taken.

15   The Milan European Council of 1985 was the first instance; with Prime Minister Craxi forcing a vote on the issue of an intergovernmental conference. This was the first time a vote was taken on such an issue and Mrs Thatcher had found herself in a minority.

16   The Italians argued that they had offered to substitute the reference to a single currency (one of the main British dislikes) in the final summit text with Europe's own currency to accommodate Britain's own proposal of a 'hard' ECU, but Mrs Thatcher had said no: the *Independent*, 21 December 1990.

17   See *Europe*. Agence Internationale d'Information pour la Presse, Luxembourg–Brussels, 5368, 12–13 November 1990.

18   There was a danger that both Denmark and Ireland would respectively hold a referendum before ratification which could delay the timetable, as they did on the SEA.

19   The UK government forwarded (in November 1990) an alternative (evolutionary) approach which excludes stages two and three of the Delors Plan. The British proposal broadly suggests 'convergence by natural forces' and envisaged 'a hard ECU' as a thirteenth currency.

20   This meant that countries like Denmark, Greece and Portugal had gone through a process of conversion and adopted a more federalist type of thinking.

21   With regard to social policy, action was urged on the implementation of the social charter, health and safety protection at work, industrial relations, vocational training, the free movement of workers, the information and consultation of workers, equal treatment for men and women, and the social dialogue.

22   Germany suggested a special voting system for social laws. If two-thirds of the MEPs voted for a law, it would take the opposition of more than one country in the Council of Ministers to stop it. This could prevent a country like Britain or Ireland from blocking the EC's social programme.

23   Ireland was worried that too many social policy decisions could make it less attractive to investors.

24   Of course, if Luxembourg abandoned the unanimity principle on tax matters, it could no longer block EC efforts to harmonise indirect taxes and thus undermine its own position of providing a 'tax haven' for foreigners.

25   There was also a question over whether Article 223 would remain in tact, which effectively excludes the application of EC competition rules in national defence industries.

26   One way to carry out majorities would be by not letting abstentions of one or several member states interfere with the final decision.

27   A point of dissension concerns whether the ambassadors to NATO would double as ambassadors to the WEU (desired by Britain) or whether the ambassadors to the Community would double as ambassadors to the WEU (preferred by France).

28   This was repeated in their joint paper of 6 February 1991.

29   The Italians also suggested that they would only ratify the new treaty on Political Union after the EP had ratified it.

30   See Herbert Simon, 'A behavioural model of rational choice', *Quarterly Journal of Economics*, LXIX, February 1955. See also Charles Lindblom, *The Policy-Making Process*, Englewood Cliffs, 1968.

31   It is interesting to note that in January 1991, the EC agreed to a Greek request for a loan of L1.5 billion to help it to overcome severe economic difficulties but on condition that tough domestic austerity measures were swiftly introduced. See the *Independent* of 29 January 1991.

32   Apparently, the French would be ready to take part fully in a NATO that had a European commander rather than, as now, an American. See the *Economist*, 15 December 1990.

33   J. P. Jacque and J. H. H. Weiler, 'On the road to european union – a new judicial architecture: an agenda for the intergovernmental conference', *Common Market Law Review*, XXVII, 2, 1990, pp. 185–203.

34   Marc Wilke and Helen Wallace, 'Subsidiarity: approaches to power-sharing in the European Community'. RIIA discussion paper no. 27, Royal Insitute for International Affairs, 1990.

35   Article 235 of the EEC Treaty gives a kind of general legislative authorisation and permits the Council of Ministers, acting unanimously, to legislate in any agreed area for which the original drafters had not seen fit to make specific provisions. Mutual recognition of national regulations is being used not only in conjunction with the free movement of goods but also in the field of financial services, university degrees, vocational training and indirect taxation. A directive, according to article 189, is binding with regard to the stipulated unions but allowing member states to choose the means of imple-

mentation. Most of the provisions adopted under the internal market programme have been directives rather than regulations which are not only binding with regard to their ends but also to their means. For further details see Renaud Dehousse, '1992 and beyond: the institutional dimension of the internal market programme', *Legal Issues of European Integration*, 1989/1, pp. 109–36.

36   European Parliament Draft Treaty Establishing the European Union, EP Directorate General for Information and Public Relations, February 1984.

37   Michael Huebel, 'European initiatives in broadcasting policy', in Carl-Christoph Schweitzer and Detler Karsten, eds, *The Federal Republic of Germany and EC Membership Evaluated*, London, 1990.

38   See House of Common Foreign Affairs Committee, Second Report on The Operation of the Single European Act.

39   An elaboration of the points raised for clarification can be found in 'Editorial comments', *Common Market Law Review*, XXVII, 2, 1990, pp. 181–4, and in Vlad Constantinesco, 'Subsidiaritaet: Zentrales Verfassungsprinzip fuer die Politische Union', *Integration*, 4/90, Bonn, 1990, pp. 165–78.

40   These possibilities are outlined in greater detail in Wilke and Wallace, 'Subsidiarity: approaches to power-sharing in the European Community'.

41   Article 100A paragraph 4 allows more stringent rules to be laid down than other countries in the Community in such areas as the environment, working conditions and health. For implications of Article 235 see note 35 above.

42   See 'Editorial comments', *Common Market Law Review*, XXVII, 2, 1990, pp. 181–4.

43   What is required at that stage is: (1) the abolition of obstacles to the free movement of capital; (2) participation of the largest possible of member states' currencies in the EMS; and (3) the existence of effective arrangements preventing, in each member state, the monetary financing of public sector budget deficits. This would ensure that the Community of the member states are not liable for the debts of another member state.

44   See Williams, 'Sovereignty and accountability', p. 302. See also chapter 5 of this book.

45   Sbragia, 'The European Community and institutional development'.

46   The EC was seen as blatantly unable, at the time of the Gulf crisis in December 1990 and January 1991, to define a political attitude and to take coherent action in the field of external politics and defence. The Community neither played the part of a mediator (not even the Iraqi Foreign Minister wanted to confer with his European colleagues in the end) nor was it able to agree on its assessment of the risks Saddam Hussein posed.

47   The decision by the Bundesbank in February 1991 to raise the German interest rate was criticised and branded as yet another case of 'Bundesbank unilateralism' and as another example of the asymmetry which exists within the EMS. See *Europe*, 6 February 1991.

48   There were worries that the EC might splinter into two or three rates

of economic development. The most advanced countries might immediately join Germany in an EMU, while the less developed or weaker economies might opt for a more gradual adhesion. For a more general analysis of a tow-speed EC, see Helen Wallace with Adam Ridley, Europe: *The Challenge of Diversity*, London, 1985.

49 See Reinhardt Rummel, 'Testing regional integration: new challenges for the community's foreign policy', unpublished paper, September 1990, p. 6.

50 See Andrew Moravcsik, 'Negotiating the Single European Act: national interests and conventional statecraft in the European Community', *International Organization*, XLV, 1, 1991, p. 48.

51 This view is in contrast to that of Moravcsik who foresaw major obstacles being placed 'in the path of attempts to extend the reform to new issues, such as monetary policy', Moravcsik, 'Negotiating the Single European Act', p. 47.

Bibliography

ALBERT, M. and BALL, R., 'Towards European economic recovery in the 1980s', Report for the European Parliament, 1983.

ALEXANDER, Willy, 'Continental Can case', *Common Market Law Review*, 10, 1973, pp. 311–9.

ALT, James, 'Crude politics: oil and the political economy of unemployment in Britain and Norway, 1970–1985', *British Journal of Political Science*, XVII, 2, 1987, pp. 149–99.

ASHOFF, Guido, 'The textile policy of the EC', *Journal of Common Market Studies*, XXII, 1, 1981, pp. 17–46.

ATTINA, Fulvio, 'Institutions and identity: rethinking European integration with a neo-institutional approach', paper delivered at the ISA Convention in London, April 1989.

AXELROD, Robert and KEOHANE, Robert O., 'Achieving cooperation under anarchy: strategies and institutions', *World Politics*, XXXVIII, 1, 1985, pp. 226–54.

BASSOMPIERRE, Guy de, *Changing the Guard in Brussels: An Insider's View of the EC Presidency*, Praeger, New York, 1988.

BOGDANOR, Vernon, *Democratising the Community*, Federal Trust for Education and Research, London, June 1990.

BOLTHO, Andrea ed., *The European Economy: Growth and Crisis*, Oxford University Press, Oxford, 1982.

BONVICINI, Gianni and REGELSBERGER, Elfriede, 'The decisionmaking process in the EC's European Council', *International Spectator*, 22, 3, July–September 1987, pp. 152–75.

BULMER, Simon, *The Domestic Structure of European Community Policy-Making in West Germany*, Garland, New York, 1986.

BULMER, Simon and PATERSON, William, *The Federal Republic of Germany and the European Community*, Allen & Unwin, London, 1987.

BULMER, Simon and WESSELS, Wolfgang, *The European Council: Decision-making in European Politics*, Macmillan, London, 1987.

die BUNDESREPUBLIK DEUTSCHLAND IN DER EUROPAISCHEN GEMEINSCHAFT 1988: Dokumentation, Auswaertiges Amt, Bonn, 1988.

CALINGAERT, Michael, *The 1992 Challenge From Europe: Development of the European Community's Internal Market*, National Planning Association, Washington DC, 1988.

CAMERON, David R., 'Sovereign states in a single market: integration and intergovernmentalism in the European Community', paper delivered at the annual meeting of the American Political Science Association, San Francisco, 30 August–2 September 1990.

CARR, Edward Hallet, *The Twenty Years Crisis, 1919–1939: An Introduction to the Study of International Relations*, Macmillan, London, 1939, 2nd edn 1964.

CECCHINI, Paolo with Michel Catinat and Alexis Jacquemin, *The European Challenge 1992. The Benefits of a Single Market* (English edition by John Robinson), Wildwood House, Aldershot, 1988.

COFFEY, Peter, *The European Monetary System: Past, Present and Future*, M. Nijhoff, Dordrecht, 1984.

COMMISSION OF THE EC, 'Solemn declaration on European union', *Bulletin of the EC*, no. 6, Brussels, 1983, pp. 24–9.

COMMISSION OF THE EC, 'Completing the internal market' (the 'White Paper'), COM (85) 310, Brussels, 14 June 1985.

COMMISSION OF THE EC, 'Single European Act', *Bulletin of the EC*, Supplement 2/86, Office for Official Publication of the EC, Luxembourg, 1986.

COMMISSION OF THE EC, 'European economy: the economics of 1992', 35, Brussels, March 1988.

COMMISSION OF THE EC, 'Twenty-second general report on the activities of the European Communities: 1988', Brussels, 1989.

COMMISSION OF THE EC, 'A Community of twelve: key figures', European File 3–4/89, Office for Official Publications of the EC, Luxembourg, March 1989.

COMMISION OF THE EC, 'Commission opinion of 21 October 1990 on the proposal for amendment of the treaty establishing the European Economic Community with a view to political union', COM (90) 600 final, Brussels, 23 October 1990.

COMMITTEE OF THREE, 'Report on European institutions', presented to the European Council, Brussels, 1979.

COMMON MARKET LAW REVIEW, 'Editorial comments', XXVII, 2, summer 1990, pp. 181–4.

CONSTANTINESCO, Vlad, 'Subsidiaritaet: zentrales verfassungsprinzip fuer die politische union', *Integration*, 4/90, Europa Union Verlag, Bonn, 1990, pp. 165–78.

CORBETT, Richard, 'Die neuen Verfahren nach der Einheitlichen Akte: Mehr Einfluss fuer das Europaeische Parlament', *Integration*, 1, Europa Union Verlag, Bonn, 1989.

CORBETT, Richard, 'Testing the new procedures: the European Parliament's first experiences with its new "Single Act" powers', *Journal of Common Market Studies*, XXVII, 4, 1989, pp. 359–72.

DALTON, Russell, *Citizen Politics in Western Democracies: Public Opinion and Political Parties in the United States, Great Britain, West Germany and France*, Chatham House Publishers, New Jersey, 1988.

DAMGAARD, E., GERLICH, P. and RICHARDSON, Jeremy, eds, *The Politics of Economic Crisis: Lessons from Western Europe*, Avebury, Aldershot, 1989.

DE VRIE, Johan K., *Political Integration: The Formation of Theory and Its Problems*, Mouton, The Hague, 1972.

DEHOUSSE, Renaud, '1992 and beyond: the institutional dimension of the internal market programme', Legal Issues of European Integration 1989/1, *Law Review of the Europa Instituut*, University of Amsterdam, pp. 109–36.

DIEHL, Paul F., ed., *The Politics of International Organizations, Patterns and Insights*, Doresy Press, Chicago, 1989.

DOLAN, Michael, 'Dialectical political economy and European integration: critique of extant theory and research design', paper presented at the ISA Convention, London, April 1989.

EDWARD, David, 'The impact of the Single Act on the institutions', *Common Market Law Review*, XXIV, 1, 1987, pp. 19–30.

EHLERMANN, Claus-Dieter, 'The institutional development of the EC under the Single European Act', *Aussen Politik*, (German foreign affairs review), XLI, 2, 1990, pp. 135–46.

EMERSON, Michael et al., *The Economics of 1992: The EC Commission's Assessment of the Economic Effects of Completing the Internal Market*, Oxford University Press, Oxford, 1988.

EUROPEAN PARLIAMENT, Draft Treaty Establishing the European Union, EP Directorate General for Information and Public Relations, Luxembourg, February 1984.

EUROPEAN PARLIAMENT, Directorate General for Research, 'The impact of the European Parliament on Community policies', Research and Documentation Papers: Action Taken Series no. 3, Luxembourg, November 1988.

EVERLING, Ulrich, 'Possibilities and limits of European integration', *Journal of Common Market Studies*, 1980, pp. 217–28.

FITZMAURICE, John, 'An analysis of the European Community's co-operation procedure', *Journal of Common Market Studies*, XXVI, 4, June 1988, pp. 389–400.

FLORA, Peter, ed., *Growth to Limits: The Western European Welfare States since World War II*, 4 vols, de Gruyter, Berlin, 1987.

GINSBERG, Roy H., *Foreign Policy Actions of the European Community. The Politics of Scale*, Adamantine Press Limited, London, 1989.

GLAESNER, H.J., 'The Single European Act', *Year Book of European Law*, 6, 1986, Oxford University Press, Oxford, 1987, pp. 283–312.

GOUREVITCH, Peter, 'The second image reversed: the international source of domestic politics', *International Organization*, XXXII, autumn 1978, pp. 881–911.

GRABITZ, Eberhard, ed., *Abgestufte Integration: eine Alternative zum herkoemlichen Integrationskonzept*, Kehl am Rhein, 1984.

GRAZIANI Report, European Parliament Session Documents, 26 September 1988.

GRIECO, Joseph, 'Anarchy and the limits of cooperation', *International*

Organization, XLII, 3, 1988, pp. 485–507.

GUNLICKS, Arthur B., ed., 'Federalism and intergovernmental relations in West Germany: a fortieth year appraisal', Publius, XIX, 4, fall 1989.

HAAS, Ernst B., *The Uniting of Europe: Political, Social, and Economic Forces, 1950–1957*, Stanford University Press, Stanford, 1958.

HAAS, Ernst B., *Beyond the Nation-State: Functionalism and International Organization*, Stanford University Press, Stanford, 1964.

HAAS, Ernst B., 'International integration. the European and the universal process', *International Political Communities. An Anthology*, Anchor Books, New York, 1966, pp. 93–129.

HAAS, Ernst B., 'The uniting of Europe and the uniting of Latin America', *Journal of Common Market Studies*, V, June 1967, pp. 315–43.

HAAS, Ernst B., 'The obsolesence of regional integration theory', Research Series 25, Institute of International Studies, Berkeley, University of California, 1975.

HARRISON, Reginald, *Europe in Question – Theories of Regional Integration*, Allen & Unwin Ltd, London, 1974.

HARTLEY, T. C., *European Community Law*, Clarendon Press, Oxford, 1983.

HAY, Peter, *Federalism and Supranational Organizations*, University of Illinois Press, 1966.

HAYES-RENSHAW, Fiona, LEQUESNE, Christian and MAYOR-LOPEZ, Pedro, 'The permanent representation of the member states of the European Communities', *Journal of Common Market Studies*, XXVIII, 2, 1989, pp. 119–37.   ˙

HERMAN, Valentine and SCHENDELEN, Rinus van, eds, *The European Parliament and the National Parliaments*, Saxon House, Westmead, 1979.

HERTJE, A., ed., *Investigating in Europe's Future*, Oxford, Blackwell, 1983.

HIRSCH, V., 'Marche interieur: une nouvelle impulsion grace a l'acte unique?', *Revue du Marche Common*, 303.

HODGES, Michael and WALLACE, William, eds, *Economic Divergence in the European Community*, Allen & Unwin, London, 1981.

HOFFMANN, Stanley, 'Obstinate or obsolete? The fate of the nation-state and the case of Western Europe', *Daedalus*, 1966, pp. 862–915.

HOFFMANN, Stanley, 'Reflections on the national state in Western Europe today', *Journal of Common Market Studies*, XXI, 1, 1982, pp. 21–37.

HOFFMANN, Stanley, 'What is at stake in the future of the nation state in Western Europe', *European Affairs*, Fall 1989.

HOSCHEIT, Jean-Marc and WESSELS, Wolfgang, eds, *The European Council 1974–1986: Evaluation and Prospects*, Institute of Public Administration, Maastricht, 1988.

HOUSE OF COMMONS, Foreign Affairs Committee, 'Operation of the Single European Act', Second Report, Session 1989–90, HMSO, London, 14 March 1990.

HOWE, SIR Geoffrey, 'Developments in the European Community: July–December 1986, the United Kingdom Presidency', (*European Com-*

munities, no. 19 [1987]), presented to Parliament by the Secretary of State for Foreign and Commonwealth Affairs, HMSO, London, April 1987.

HU, Yao-su, *Europe Under Stress*, Butterworth, London, 1981.

HUEBEL, Michael, 'European initiatives in broadcasting policy', in Carl-Christoph Schweitzer and Deter Karsten, eds, *The Federal Republic of Germany and EC membership evaluated*, Pinter Publishers, London, 1990.

HURD, Douglas, 'Developments in the European Community: July–December 1989' (*European Communities*, No. 17 [1990]), presented to Parliament by the Secretary of State for Foreign and Commonwealth Affairs, HMSO, London, April 1990.

HURWITZ, Leon, *The European Community and the Management of International Cooperation*, Greenwood Press, New York, 1987.

JACQUE, Jean Paul and WEILER, Joseph H. H., 'On the road to European union – a new judicial architecture: an agenda for the Intergovernmental Conference', *Common Market Law Review*, XXVII, 2, 1990, pp. 185–203.

JONES, Walter S., *The Logic of International Relations*, 6th edition, Scott, Foresman and Co., Boston, 1988.

JORDAN, R. and FELD, W., Europe in the Balance. *The Changing Contest of European International Politics*, Faber & Faber Ltd, London and Boston, 1986.

KAISER, Karl, MERLINI, Cesare, MONTBRIAL, Tierry de, WELLENSTEIN, Edmund and WALLACE, William, 'The European Community: progress or decline?', report published in the UK by the Royal Institute of International Affairs, London, 1983.

KATZENSTEIN, Peter, ed., *Between Power and Plenty: Foreign Economic Policies of Advanced Industrial States*, University of Wisconsin Press, Madison, 1978.

KATZENSTEIN, Peter, *Small States in World Markets: Industrial Policy in Europe*, Cornell University Press, Ithaca and London, 1985.

KEOHANE, Robert O., 'The demand for international regimes', *International Organization*, XXXVI, 2, 1982, pp. 141–71.

KEOHANE, Robert O., 'International institutions: two approaches', *International Studies Quarterly*, XXXII, 1988.

KEOHANE, Robert O. and HOFFMANN, Stanley, 'European Community politics and institutional change', revised version of paper prepared for Florence workshop on the Dynamics of European Integration, 10/12 September 1989, 3 November 1989.

KEOHANE, Robert O. and NYE Joseph S., *Power and Interdependence: World Politics in Transition*, Little, Brown and Co., Boston 1977.

KIRCHNER, Emil J., *Trade Unions as a Pressure Group in the European Community*, Saxon House, Westmead, 1977.

KIRCHNER, Emil J., 'Has the Single European Act opened the door for a European security policy?', *Journal of European Integration*, XIII, 1, 1989, pp. 1–14.

KIRCHNER, Emil J. and STEFANOU, Constantin, 'Institutional implications of European integration', *Saint Louis University Public Law*

Review, IX, 1, 1990, pp. 61–82.

KRASNER, Stephen, ed., *International Regimes*, Cornell University Press, Ithaca, 1983.

KRISLOV, Samuel, EHLERMANN, Claus-Dieter and WEILER, Joseph, 'The political organs and the decision-making process in the United States and the European Community', *Integration Through Law: Europe and the American Federal Experience*, European University Institute, Florence, Walter de Gruyter, Berlin, 1986.

LEQUESNE, Christian, 'Europapolitik unter Mitterrand: die franzoesische Praesidentschaft als Etappenziel', *Integration*, 4/89, Europa Union Verlag, Bonn, 1989, pp. 152–61.

LEVI, Lucio, 'Recent developments in federalist theory', *The Federalist*, 2, 1987.

LINDBERG, Leon, *The Political Dynamics of European Economic Integration*, Stanford, 1963.

LINDBERG, Leon and SCHEINGOLD, Stuart, *Europe's Would-be Polity*, Prentice-Hall, Englewood Cliffs, 1970.

LINDBERG, Leon and SCHEINGOLD, Stuart, eds, *Regional Integration: Theory and Research*, Harvard University Press, Harvard, 1971.

LINDBLOM, Charles, *The Policy-Making Process*, Prentice Hall, Englewood Cliffs, 1968.

LODGE, Juliet, 'The Single European Act: towards a new dynamism', *Journal of Common Market Studies*, XXIV, 3, 1985, pp. 203–23.

LODGE, Juliet, 'The Single European Act and the new legislative cooperation procedure: a critical analysis', *Journal of European Integration*, XI, 1, 1987, pp. 5–28.

LODGE, Juliet, 'Social policy', *Journal of European Integration*, XIII, 1990, pp. 135–50.

LUDLOW, Peter, *The Making of the European Monetary System: a Case Study of the Politics of the European Community*, Butterworth Scientific, London, Boston, 1982.

MERLINI, Cesare, ed., *Economic Summits and Western Decision-Making*, Croom Helm, London, 1984.

MILWARD, Alan S., *The Reconstruction of Western Europe 1945–1951*, Methuen, London, 1987.

MITRANY, David, *A Working Peace System*, Quadrangle, Chicago, 1966.

MORAVCSIK, Andrew, 'Negotiating the Single European Act: national interests and conventional statecraft in the European Community', *International Organization*, XLV, 1, 1991, pp. 19–56.

MORGAN, Annette, 'From summit to Council: evolution in the EEC', European series 27, Chatham House, the Royal Institute of International Affairs, Political and Economic Planning, London, June 1976.

MORGENTHAU, Hans J., *Politics Among Nations: The Struggle for Power and Peace*, 5th edition, Knopf, New York, 1973.

NEUNREITHER, Karlheinz, 'Application of the Single European Act: emergence of a new institutional triangle', paper presented at the Fourteenth World Congress of the International Political Science Association, Washington DC, 28 August–1 September 1988.

NICOLL, William, 'Paths to European union', *Journal of Common Market Studies*, XXIII, 3, March 1985, pp. 199–206.

NICOLL, William, 'Les procedures Luns/Westerterp pour l'information du Parlement europeen', *Revue du Marche Common*, 300, 1986, pp. 475–6.

NICOLL, William and SALMON, Trevor, Understanding the European Communities, Philip Allan, London, 1990.

NOEL, Emile, *Working Together: The Institutions of the European Community*, Office for Official Publications of the European Communities, Luxembourg, 1988.

NYE, Joseph, *Peace in Parts: Integration and Conflict in Regional Organisation*, Little, Brown and Co., Boston, 1971.

OECD, 'Science and technology indicators II, R&D, invention and competitiveness', Paris, 1986.

OFFICE FOR OFFICIAL PUBLICATIONS OF THE EUROPEAN COMMUNITIES, *Europe in Figures*, Luxembourg, 1988.

OFFICIAL JOURNAL OF THE EUROPEAN COMMUNITIES. *Debates of the European Parliament*, Office for Offical Publications of the EC, Luxembourg.

O NUALLAIN, Colm, ed., with HOSCHEIT, Jean-Marc, *The Presidency of the European Council of Ministers: Impacts and Implications for National Governments*, Croom Helm, London, 1985.

PADOA-SCHIOPPA, Tommaso with Michael Emerson, Mervyn King, Jean-Claude Milleron, Jean Paelinck, Lucas Papademos, Alfredo Pastor and Fritz Scharpf, Efficiency, *Stability and Equality: A Strategy for the Evolution of the Economic System of the European Community* (a report by), Oxford University Press, Oxford, 1987.

PELKMANS, Jacques and WINTERS, Alan, 'Europe's domestic market', Chatham House Papers 43, Routledge, London, 1987.

PENTLAND, Charles, *International Theory and European Integration*, Faber & Faber Ltd, London, 1973.

PESCATORE, Pierre, 'Some critical remarks on the Single European Act', *Common Market Law Review*, XXIV, 1, 1987, pp. 9–18.

PICHT, Robert, 'Deutsch-franzoesische beziehungen nach dem fall der mauer: angst vor "Grossdeutschland"?', *Integration*, 2/90, Europa Union Verlag, Bonn, April 1990, pp. 47–58.

PIJPERS, Alfred, REGELSBERGER, Elfriede and WESSELS, Wolfgang, eds, in collaboration with Geoffrey Edwards, *European Political Cooperation in the 1980s: a Common Foreign Policy for Western Europe*, M. Nijhoff, Dordrecht, 1988.

PRICE, Roy, ed., *The Dynamics of European Union*, Croom Helm, London, 1987.

PUTNAM, Robert, 'Diplomacy and domestic politics: the logic of two-level games', *International Organization*, XLII, 1988, pp. 427–60.

RESEARCH GROUP on European Affairs headed by Werner Weidenfeld, 'European deficits, European perspectives – taking stock for tomorrow', published by the Bertelsmann Foundation, Guetersloh, 1989.

ROCHESTER, Martin, 'The rise and fall of international organisation as a field of study, *International Organization*, 1986, pp. 777–813.

ROSS, George; HOFFMANN, Stanley and MALZACHER, Sylvia, eds, *The Mitterrand Experiment: Continuity and Change in Modern France*, Polity Press, Cambridge, 1987.

RUMMEL, Reinhardt, 'Testing regional integration: new challenges for the Community's foreign policy', unpublished paper, SWP, Ebenhausen, 15 September 1990.

SANDHOLTZ, Wayne and ZYSMANN, John, 'Recasting the EC bargain', *World Politics*, XLII, 1989, pp. 95–128.

SASSE, Christoph, POULLET, Edourd, COOMBES, David and DEPREZ, Gerard, *Decision Making in the European Community*, Praeger, New York, 1977.

SBRAGIA, Alberta, 'The European Community and institutional development: politics, money and law', paper prepared for the Brookings Institution's Conference on 'European Political Institutions and Policymaking After 1992', 29–30 March 1990.

SCHARPF, Fritz, 'The joint-decision trap: lessons from German federalism and European integration', *Public Administration*, 66, autumn 1988, pp. 239–78.

SCHEEL, Walter, 'Die EG nach der deutschen Prasidentschaft – 1992 ist nather geruckt', *Integration*, 4/88, Europa Union Verlag, 1988, pp. 143–9.

SCHMIDT, Peter, 'The Franco–German Defence and Security Council', *Aussen Politik*, (German foreign affairs review), XL, 4, 1989, pp. 360–71.

SCHMUCK, Otto, 'Integrationsschub durch neuen Vertrag? Reformperspektiven im Vorfeld des Mailander Gipfels', *Integration*, 2/85, Europa Union Verlag, Bonn, April 1985.

SCHNEIDER, Heinrich, 'Rueckblick fuer die Zukunft – Konzeptionelle Weichenstellungen fur die Europaeische Einigung', *Europaeische Schriften*, 63, Europa Union Verlag, Bonn, 1986.

SELBERT, Roger B., 'Compatible two sphere integration: the simultaneous Danish participation in the European Communities and Nordic cooperation', published with the Commission of the European Communities, Brussels, 1979.

SHARP, Margaret and SHEARMAN, Claire, 'European technological collaboration', Chatham House Papers 36, Routledge & Kegan Paul, London, 1987.

SIMON, Herbert, 'A behavioural model rational choice', *Quarterly Journal of Economics*, LXIX, February 1955, pp. 99–118.

STATIONERY OFFICE, DUBLIN, *Irish Presidency of the European Communities – January–June 1990*, Stationery Office, Dublin, 1990.

STATISTICAL OFFICE OF THE EC, 'Government financing of research and development 1980–1987', *Eurostat*, basic statistics of the Community, Luxembourg, 1989.

TAYLOR, Paul, *The Limits of European Integration*, Croom Helm, London, 1983.

THIEL, Elke, 'Conflict and cooperation: US–European economic relations' *Aussen Politik*, (German foreign affairs review), XL, 3, 1989, pp. 264–76.

THIEL, Elke, 'From the internal market to an economic and monetary

Bibliography 159

union', *Aussen Politik*, (German foreign affairs review), XL, 1, 1989, pp. 66–75.

TINDEMANS, Leo, 'Report on European union', *Bulletin of the European Communities*, Supplement 1/76, Brussels, 1976.

TROY JOHNSTON, Mary, 'The European Council: an integrative or desintegrative innovation', paper delivered at the European Community Studies Association inaugural conference, Washington, May 1989.

TSOUKALIS, Loukas, *The Politics and Economics of European Monetary Integration*, Allen & Unwin, London, 1977.

TSOUKALIS, Loukas and STRAUSS, Rober, 'Crisis and adjustment in European steel: beyond laisser-faire', *Journal of Common Market Studies*, XXIII, 3, March 1985, pp. 207–28.

TSOUKALIS, Loukas, ed., Europe, *America and the World Economy*, Basil Blackwell, Oxford, 1986.

UNGERER, Werner, 'EC progress under the German Presidency', *Aussen Politik*, XXXIX, 4, 1988, pp. 311–22.

UNGERER, Werner, 'Die neuen Verfahren nach der Einheitlichen Europaeischen Akte: Eine Bilanz aus der Ratsperspektive', *Integration*, 3, Europa Union Verlag, Bonn, 1989.

VEDEL REPORT, *Bulletin of the European Communities*, Supplement 4/72, Brussels, 1972.

VORNBAEUMEN, Axel, 'Dynamik in der Zwangsjacke. Die Praesidentschaft im Ministerrat der Europaeischen Gemeinschaft als Fuehrungsinstrument', Mainzer Beitraege zur Europaeischen Einigung, Herausgegeben von Werner Weidenfeld, V, Europa Union Verlag, 1985.

WALLACE, Helen and EDWARDS, Geoffrey, 'European Community: the evolving role of the Presidency of the Council', *International Affairs*, Royal Institute of International Affairs, October 1976, pp. 535–50.

WALLACE, Helen, WALLACE, William and WEBB, Carole, eds, *Policy Making in the European Communities*, John Wiley and Sons, Chichester, 1977.

WALLACE, Helen with RIDLEY, Adam, 'Europe: the challenge of diversity', Chatham House Papers 29, Routledge & Kegan Paul, London, 1985.

WALLACE, William, 'Europe as a confederation: the Community and the nation state', *Journal of Common Market Studies*, XXI, 1, 1982, pp. 57–68.

WALLACE, William, 'The Tranformation of Western Europe', Chatham House Papers, Pinter Publishers, London, 1990.

WALLACE, William, ed., *The Dynamics of European Integration*, Pinter Publishers, London, 1990.

WALTZ, Kenneth N., *Man, the State and War: A Theoretical Analysis*, Columbia University Press, New York, 1959.

WARD, Hugh and EDWARDS, Geoffrey, 'Chicken and technology: the politics of the EC's budget for research and development', *Review of International Studies*, XVI, 1990, pp. 111–31.

WEILER, Joseph, 'Community, member states and European integration: is the law relevant', *Journal of Common Market Studies*, XXI, 1, 1982, pp.

39–56.

WESSELS, Wolfgang, 'Die Einheitliche Europaische Akte – Zementierung des status quo order Einstieg in die Europaische Union?', *Integration*, 2/86, Europa Union Verlag, Bonn, 1986, pp. 65–79.

WESSELS, Wolfgang, 'The growth of the EC system – a product of the dynamics of modern European states? A plea for a more comprehensive approach', paper delivered at the VIVth World Congress of the International Political Science Association, Washington DC, 28 August–1 September 1988.

WESSELS, Wolfgang and REGELSBERGER, Elfriede, eds, *The Federal Republic of Germany and the European Community: The Presidency and Beyond*, published as no. 2 of the series Analysesof European Policies by the Institut fur Europaische Politik, Europa Union Verlag, Bonn, 1988.

WESSELS, Wolfgang and WEIDENFELD, Werner, eds, *Jahrbuch Europaische Integration 1987/88*, Bonn, 1988.

WHEARE, Kenneth Clinton, *Federal Governments*, 4th edition, Oxford University Press, London, 1963.

WILKE, Marc and WALLACE, Helen, 'Subsidiarity: approaches to power-sharing in the European Community', the Royal Institute of International Affairs discussion papers 27, Chatham House, London, 1990.

WILLIAMS, Shirley, 'Sovereignty and accountability in the European Community', *Political Quarterly*, LXI, 3, 1990, pp. 299–317.

WOODS, Stanley, 'Western Europe: technology and the future', Atlantic Paper 63, the Atlantic Institute for International Affairs, Croom Helm, London, 1987.

YOUNG, Oran R., 'International regimes: problems of concept formation', *World Politics*, XXXII, 1980.

ZYSMANN, John, *Governments, Markets and Growth – Financial Systems and the Politics of Industrial Change*, Cornell University Press, Ithaca and London, 1983.

Index